Making Twig Furniture
& HOUSEHOLD THINGS

Making Twig Furniture

& HOUSEHOLD THINGS

by Abby Ruoff

Hartley & Marks

PUBLISHERS

HARTLEY & MARKS PUBLISHERS INC.
Box 147, Point Roberts, WA 98281
3661 West Broadway, Vancouver, BC, V6R 2B8

Typeset by the Typeworks
Printed and bound in the USA

If not available at your local bookstore,
this book may be ordered from the publisher.
Send the cover price plus three dollars fifty
for shipping and handling to the appropriate
address above.

ISBN 0-88179-120-2

To Carl, who walks the woods with me

Contents

CHAPTER 5   HOUSEHOLD THINGS

CHAPTER 6   GARDEN ACCESSORIES

CHAPTER 7   BARK AND VINE PROJECTS

Making Twig Furniture

& HOUSEHOLD THINGS

INTRODUCTION

As a city kid I had the best of both worlds, spending winters in New York City and summers at my grandparents' summer home in the Catskill Mountains of New York State. The front porch of the Victorian country house held large green rockers, where the adults gathered on cool summer evenings. I, however, preferred the side porch with the twig chairs. The familiar natural form of the twigs allowed my imagination to run free. I pretended that the limbs grew into chairs by themselves, and that the elves who lived in the woods would come to sit on the chairs when I was asleep.

As an adult, I began building pieces for my own use when the need for new furniture arose, much like the early twig furniture makers. My husband Carl and I wanted to decorate our vacation home with rustic twig furniture, but we decided to build our own when we realized the high prices of both new and antique pieces. My background in design and furniture styles, combined with Carl's knowledge of woods and his expertise with woodworking, made our first project—the Armchair —fun and exciting. As time permitted, other pieces followed, and the results enhanced our cottage. In building twig furniture, I discovered a practical expression for my creative urges and renewed my interest in natural materials. I soon came to realize that I enjoy finding the materials just as much or even more than the actual building. Gathering the wood often becomes an opportunity for a late autumn or early winter picnic, and it is exciting to find the right forked branch or a curved willow limb. Building twig furniture has turned out to be a joy from start to finish.

Our furniture became a big hit with friends and neighbors, many of whom wanted to buy pieces for their own use. Soon the demand became too great, and I did not have the time to devote to building furniture on such a large scale. Instead, I decided to draw up simple plans to give to those who were interested in building their own twig furniture.

Everyone who saw these designs seemed to love them. Twig furniture is part and parcel of North America's history, and seeing it helps to stir up people's memories of rural design. At the same time, this craft's natural forms blended perfectly with the sophisticated country look that was finding its rightful place in contemporary home decorating. The appeal of twig furniture was catching on, and I soon realized that these whimsical, carefully crafted pieces were gracing some of the most lavish homes. It seemed only natural to me that there would also be a demand for do-it-yourself plans, to allow those with moderate means some of this rustic charm. Thus was created the small mail-order furniture plan business that I called Wood-Lot Farms. The volume of my mail indicated that many people had the desire to build their own twig furniture, but lacked either the confidence or the basic knowledge of carpentry to begin building without predrawn plans. My little mail-order business became a timely success. Soon some of the big home and decorating magazines (*Better Homes and Gardens, House Beautiful, Home Magazine*, and Time Life Books) began to contact me to design and build prototypes for exclusive pieces for their readers. I began writing articles as well, and seeing everything "in twig": baby cradles, picture frames, bird feeders, trays, modesty screens, and lamps. It was not long before articles about my work began to appear in such magazines as *Harrowsmith, New Choices, New York Alive*, and *Ulster*. I soon realized that other natural elements could also be incorporated, and even such humble materials as tree bark, roots, and vines have added new dimensions to my twig work.

As the twentieth century draws to a close, demand for natural furnishings is increasing. In this high-tech age, natural materials are a sight for sore eyes, with none of the unpleasant effects of synthetic materials (for example, adhesives, laminates, and plastics that may emit toxic chemicals). Using the plans in this book, and the gnarled, twisted limbs of trees, you can fashion lasting pieces of natural furniture and create your own North American classics.

This book is intended to inspire you to enjoy the creative process, to help you learn the basic techniques, and to encourage you to create your own designs. Remember, it is only a guide—because every piece of wood has a different shape, every piece you make will be an original. All you need to get started is a bundle of twigs, a few hand tools, some nails, and a sense of adventure!

HISTORY

The origins of rustic twig furniture are almost as varied as the individual pieces and the artisans who created them. Many theories surround the beginnings of this type of furniture; some are fact, while others incorporate local legend and lore. Tracing the actual beginning of rustic furniture making would be akin to pinpointing the inventor of the wheel. My research leads me to believe that various peoples have incorporated twigs and "rustic work" into their lifestyles, first out of need and then for embellishment.

Some of the earliest recorded pieces of rustic twig furniture can be traced to China, where examples are found in tenth-century paintings. *A New Book of Chinese Designs*, published in England in 1754, includes several designs for twig work.

An Appalachian region legend relates the tale of a weary traveller, tired after a long day of hiking, who came upon a riverbank and willow thicket. To aid his rest, he quickly fashioned himself a willow chair. Although this is a nice story, I am almost certain that the weary traveller probably just sat down along the edge of the river and soaked his feet.

Many craftspeople credit Native Americans as the first people to use twigs and bark for practical purposes. It is true that Native Americans used available natural materials, but it is also clear that many other groups and individuals throughout history have contributed to this style of furnishing.

Traditionally, native peoples of many nations have harvested the willow twigs that grow in abundance along riverbanks and creek beds. The supple young shoots curve when they are green and harden when dry, making willow invaluable for fashioning utilitarian items such as cradle carriers, log carriers, fish traps, and baskets. When we see a parent carrying a child in a metal-framed back carrier, we can be certain that the modern-day convenience was once made with bent willow twigs and laced hide.

The peeled bark of birch trees was used to create vessels and troughs of various sizes, ranging from small drinking cups to canoes. Native Americans, using available and renewable natural resources, can be credited with some of the finest uses of twig and bark craft. Evidence suggests that as the centuries passed, and Native Americans were forced to earn their livelihoods within the new society's cash system, they played a role in the development of rustic furniture. Some fine examples of chairs with rawhide webbing for seats and backs still exist today. These are similar in construction to snowshoes, an item believed to originate with Native American guides.

The subsequent Victorian era, and its romanticized vision of nature, created the perfect setting for rustic work. Here one could control nature and combine it with the comforts of civilization. American Victorian artists often turned to nature for inspiration, as in the paintings of the Hudson River School by such artists as Frederick Church and Thomas Cole.

British and American landscape and garden designers began to realize the virtues of the back-to-nature movement. They often placed seats of twisted, gnarled rhododendron and laurel throughout the private and public gardens popular in the middle 1800s. Perhaps the finest example can be found in New York's Central Park, where Frederick Law Olmsted and Calvert Vaux designed shelters, seats, arbors, and bridges out of twigs. Central Park was heralded at its inception as a triumph of man's ability to control nature. While cities were thought to be necessary for the growth of the nation, city dwellers, strained under artificial conditions, believed they required contact with nature to lead healthy, moral lives. Much of the rustic furniture built at this time (1830–1860) is referred to as "Gothic." It utilized burls and roots, as well as other natural gnarls, and is in great demand today by collectors.

The second half of the nineteenth century might well be called the Golden Age of rustic furnishings, for it was during this period that large summer mansions and grand resorts were built for the wealthy. From the hot springs resorts of Arkansas, Alabama, Kentucky, and Virginia, to the mountain retreats of the Great Smokies and the Adirondacks, rustic twig furniture was a fashionable interpretation of the back-to-nature movement, preached by such notables as William Cullen Bryant, then editor of *The New York Post*, and John Burroughs, a famous naturalist. Lake Mohonk, in the Shawangunk Mountains of southern New York State, advertised tranquillity and peace with nature in addition to "rustic seats with straw-thatched roofs."

Fine hotels and "Great Camps" helped to create yet another industry— tourism—and with it an outlet for twig furnishings. Local craftspeople, anxious to earn extra money, found a ready market for rustic work in the summer tourists, who liked to bring a piece of "country" home to the city.

Women's magazines of the 1800s suggested "twigwork" as a pastime for "winterwork," giving directions for picture frames, flower holders, and sewing stands. Searching through old photographs taken in many parts of the world at this time, one can find twig chairs, benches, and fences used as photographers' props for formal studio portraits.

During the late 1800s most towns had photography studios where ordinary people went to be photographed. Millions of people, both famous and obscure, had their portraits done. Using fashionable furniture props, the photographer created an illusion of equality for all, even if only on film. These early photographs are important examples of trends, as rustic twig furniture props appear to have been plentiful during the late 1800s and early 1900s. Looking through old studio photographs and tintypes, I have found examples of early twig furniture from Odessa to Omaha and in many locations in between.

The economic conditions of the Depression era gave rise to what we know as "Gypsy" twig furniture. Some of it was actually produced by Gypsies, who would hastily nail together a chair or smoking stand to earn a few cents when passing through an area. The Occasional Chair and Settee in my plans are based on Gypsy designs. Most authorities on the subject credit the creation of tripod tables and planters to the Gypsies. I have, however, found some surviving pieces of this type in Florida, and believe they were built by the Seminoles for the tourist trade during the 1920s and 1930s.

During the Depression, many state governments realized the job possibilities inherent in a willow furniture-building industry, and planted stands of willow for furniture makers to harvest. These stands were also used as a soil erosion control measure along stream banks just prior to World War II. This proved to be a short-lived enterprise, however, and most willow thickets were left unharvested. After the war years, rustic furniture went out of fashion. Wicker from the Orient was plentiful and inexpensive, and became its successor for use in summer homes and on country porches.

It was only natural that someone at some point in history would see the potential for mass-produced twig products and build a factory. The first and most productive of these factories was, and still is, The Old Hickory Furniture Company in Shelbyville, Indiana. It produces rustic furnishings out of hickory.

Competitors were quick to spring up as the demand for rustic furniture increased during the early 1900s. Records exist from this period of small factories, often only two-person operations, from New England and the Adirondacks, north to Toronto, Ontario.

Much of the factory-built furniture survives to this day, a tribute to its quality and construction. The best examples of rustic furniture, however, are the one-of-a-kind pieces made by people with little or no formal training, who took pride in their workmanship and possessed a desire to create.

The Indiana State Farm Prison in Putnamville began training inmates to build rustic hickory furniture for state agencies in 1929. The training shops remain in operation today. While the furniture is available for purchase, it can be sold under federal law only within Indiana.

The Amish people are yet another important group in the development of twig furniture. Like Shaker furniture, Amish chairs are a marriage of form and function. Examples of Amish chairs date back to the late 1800s. The basic frame is usually made of hickory, with backrests and seats of tapered branches of milled oak or ash. The slope of the chair back is an engineering feat in comfort as well as design. Many of these designs are being produced today, some by Amish furniture builders in Ohio and Pennsylvania, and others by large furniture manufacturers.

Rustic furniture has flourished throughout history. It seems fitting now that technological advances, expanding metropolitan growth, and the proliferation of man-made materials would give rise to a rustic revolution at the end of the twentieth century.

CHAPTER 1

Decorating with Twig Furniture

Furnishings that endure are a link with the past, and using them in a new way—particularly when you begin with a good design—makes them even better. If one word can be found to best describe today's interior designs it would have to be "eclectic." By combining various styles and periods, designers and homeowners alike have discovered the beauty of original, personal rooms. Even if everything in a room is new, it should not look like it was transferred from the furniture showroom to the living room. Each piece lends its own character to a room, and nothing brings more personality to a home than a handcrafted item, lovingly fashioned to transcend the passage of time.

Of course, the notion of mixing styles is not new. Homeowners have always combined styles by adding new purchases to inherited pieces. Traditionally, when the younger generation moved into the family home and combined their "modern" pieces with existing furnishings, the result became eclectic, though not by choice. This marriage of styles and periods has helped create many of today's most comfortable rooms.

Twig furniture, with its natural bends and whimsical curlicues, adds a light touch to the most serious room, and helps impart warmth to a sleek, modern interior. The natural beauty of twigs and sticks fashioned into furnishings evokes nostalgic feelings, and is just as comforting in a city apartment as in a rustic cabin.

When attempting to incorporate twig furnishings into a room, begin by deciding what piece or accessory is needed. Then think in terms of "twig." As you look around your house, you will discover that a piece of rustic twig furniture can fit in almost anywhere. Once you master the art of making it yourself, this personal addition to your home will be displayed with pride. Analyze your room when you consider what new piece you would like to add. Plan your first piece as an accent rather than a showstopper—for example, a mirror frame in the bathroom, a plant stand in the den, or a vine lampshade in the living room.

TWIG FURNISHINGS IN THE BATHROOM

Family and guest bathrooms, with their modern interiors, lend themselves beautifully to the natural charm of a few rustic accents.

Vine and Bark Baskets
These are decorative as well as useful to hold and hide the accumulation of daily toiletry needs, such as hair dryers, cosmetics, and that extra bar of soap and roll of toilet tissue.

Picture Frames
These are wonderful to accent a mirror hanging over the sink. For an easier version, simply hang a mirror on the wall and tack twigs and branches to the wall with small staples, surrounding the mirror with a natural frame. Unfortunately, this will not work on tile walls.

Plate Stand
This piece works very well for holding extra towels, as does the plant stand.

Five-Sided Cube
This can become a hamper if you change the dimensions. It is also very nice for storing towels, bath mats, and toiletries. Turned upside down, the cube can hide cleaning supplies, and, when fitted with a terrycloth cushion, it serves as a comfortable, sturdy dressing stool.

Magazine Rack
This can be used not only for magazines and books, but also for extra towels.

Towel Bar and Curtain Rod
These can be fashioned easily from straight twigs with forked branches as sup-

ports. Simply cut two twigs, approximately 6" long, each with a fork for the brackets. Drill two or three pilot holes in each bracket twig at the location where it will be attached to the wall (through the studs) or to the window frame. Cut a twig pole to the desired length for the curtain rod or towel bar. Install the pole by simply resting it across the forked twigs.

TWIG FURNISHINGS IN THE BEDROOM

I have seen many beautiful beds built out of twigs, and their natural beauty adds romantic charm to any bedroom. I would, however, suggest such a project for only the most accomplished woodworker because of the many parts and precise construction necessary to accommodate a box spring and mattress. For a similar effect, you can modify the loveseat pattern to make a headboard by attaching the arched back to the seat support beam and then adding shortened supports to the seat support beam. Add two legs and attach to the frame or wall.

Plant Stand and Plate Rack
In addition to holding plants, these pieces can also be used to hold books and magazines, for handy bedside reading.

Chairs and Loveseat
These are a perfect addition to bedrooms, especially when cushions and pillows to coordinate with the bedspreads or wallpaper are added.

Bark Baskets
These make excellent wastebaskets or flower containers. You might consider covering a wooden cheese box with sheets of bark to hold socks, handkerchiefs, or dresser-top clutter.

Window Treatments
Instead of curtains, an interesting window treatment can be used to ensure privacy and control light. Install wooden shutters intended to hold fabric inserts (or old shutters with louvers removed) and insert twigs in the openings. Light is controlled by opening and closing the shutters, rather than by adjusting the louvers. The shutters can be painted or left in their natural state. Instead of a valance, drape supple vines and twigs across the top of the window frames and tack them in place. For a more permanent installation, the vines and branches can be nailed or glued to a wooden cornice.

Attaching pine cones and acorns with glue will add interest, fresh as the forest floor.

Five-Sided Cube

This can be used to hold an extra blanket or, when turned over, can serve as a bed-side table. Three of them lined up on their sides under a window can serve as both a plant stand and a place to store magazines or other odds and ends.

Vine Shade

These impart a soothing evening glow to the bedroom. You might consider painting the shade to blend in with the room's color scheme, or adding a shocking, unexpected accent, such as a hot pink shade in an earth-toned room, or a bright orange shade in a bedroom with blue and white country checks.

Screen

With fabric inserts, a screen can stand in front of a window to hide an unsightly view or to afford privacy. You can also decorate a screen with coordinating fabric and use it as a headboard.

DINING ROOM DECORATING

Of course, the first requisite for the dining room or kitchen is a table and chairs. A dining room table made entirely of twigs is highly impractical. However, log legs fastened to a flat-surfaced top can make a useful and sturdy table. The top can vary from a used and weathered door to a stainless steel laminated surface or painted plywood board. Using twig chairs around a sleek, glass-topped, contemporary table creates an eclectic look. Once you start thinking of mixing, not matching, your options become limitless.

Vine and Bark Baskets

Baskets are perfect for serving dry snacks at a party, or for holding silverware and napkins at an informal buffet dinner. These are easy to make, and you can create any size of container you desire. The bark napkin rings give a rugged feel to even the most elegant table.

Vine Shade

While nice on lamps, vine shades are truly unique when used as hanging shades over a dining table.

USING TWIGS IN THE KITCHEN

My kitchen table is made of beech legs that are three inches in diameter and a maple butcher-block top. Rather than ruin the top by screwing or nailing the legs through the surface, I fastened the legs to the underside using metal L-braces intended as shelf supports. The braces are fastened to each leg at the inside corner, and so are not noticeable. Many styles of chairs will fit nicely around such a table. You might want to use a variety, placing two twig chairs at the ends, and twig or picnic benches at the sides. Shaker-style ladder-backs or an assortment of painted chairs would also look nice.

Standing Planter
Add a wooden or Plexiglas shelf to the bottom, and use the standing planter to store wine or to hold cookbooks.

Five-Sided Cube
Line the cube with a large bag and place it on top of the refrigerator or in an un-used corner to collect recyclable bottles and cans.

Basket Planter
Filled with fruit, this becomes a charming centerpiece for the kitchen table. Place an early tomato harvest in the basket, and while they ripen you will have a charm-ing arrangement. Basket planters are also handy for storing potatoes and onions when hung from a Shaker-style peg rack.

An otherwise dreary kitchen can easily be brightened by adding a few simple accents. Hang twig-framed fruit or vegetable prints, or a grapevine wreath trimmed with dried herbs and roadside wildflowers. Simple trivets and napkin rings can be woven out of vines or supple thin twigs. Hanging vine shades over the lights above a kitchen island is another easy way to add warmth.

RUSTIC ACCENTS IN THE LIVING ROOM AND DEN

Unless you are trying to duplicate the authentic charm of a country camp, you probably will not want to fill an entire room with twig furniture. For daily living, most people prefer modern comfort alongside graceful and informal twig pieces.

The loveseat, or any one of the chairs, would be a perfect addition to the living room, and they become surprisingly comfortable when cushions are added.

Good choices for fabric to cover the cushions include rag rugs (new or used), pieces of quilts, remnants of Oriental rugs, vintage bark cloth drapery fabric, and white Marseilles bedspreads. Never pass up worn fabrics or rugs at house sales or auctions if there are usable sections that can be transformed into wonderful one-of-a-kind pillows or cushions for your twig furniture. With new fabrics, you are limited only by the extent of your imagination. Gingham checks, mattress ticking (white or tea-dyed), chintz, leather, suede, handwoven or reproduction coverlets, linen, or white duck all look lovely on twig furniture, depending on the room setting.

Five-Sided Cube

This versatile cube is great for holding logs near the hearth, magazines by the sofa, or large plants near a sunny window. When turned over, with a cushion resting on top, the cube makes a wonderful ottoman. I have also used two of them as a coffee table base with a large, thick piece of glass placed on top of them.

Child's Chair

The child's ladder-back chair in our living room awaits small visitors, but also serves as a book or plant stand when not in use. Even where there are no children, this miniature chair evokes warm thoughts of "home" and "family."

TWIG FURNITURE IN AN OUTDOOR SETTING: PORCHES, DECKS, AND PATIOS

Twig furniture is used indoors so often that I want to emphasize how suitable it is for outdoor use. Today's eclectic styles of decorating, and the trend toward casual outdoor entertaining, combine to form the perfect setting for twig furniture. It mixes nicely with other natural styles of outdoor furniture and brings a fresh new spirit to outdoor entertaining.

When we needed a large outdoor table for our covered veranda, we cut four sturdy cedar poles, five inches each in diameter and held together by two sturdy braces, and fastened them to the underside of a silver-grey, weathered cellar door.

MAINTENANCE

As with any type of furniture, it is important to know a few simple maintenance rules. If you are using twig furniture out-of-doors, check periodically for insect activity. If you find tiny, pin-sized holes in the wood, check for sawdust on the floor beneath the furniture. If insects are present, first try washing the piece with soapy water. Check again for insects at least once a week and, if the problem is not cured, treat the piece with a safe insecticide spray. Many natural sprays can be purchased at a garden center specifically for this use. Often they come in powder form and can be mixed with water and applied with a plant mister. For more information—see page 19 "How To Examine the Twigs for Larvae."

If your furniture is placed on a covered porch, it requires very little care and can be used for many years. Simply replace the cushions whenever desired. If, however, your outdoor area is a deck or patio, and your furniture is subjected to the elements, it will take a bit more effort to preserve it. Coat the wood with a clear varnish, such as polyurethane or tungseed oil, in order to keep the bark intact. With this protection, your furniture will last for years on the deck or in the garden. In areas where winter is harsh, store outdoor pieces in a protected place when not in use.

PAINTED TWIG FURNITURE

While most new and antique twig furniture is left in its natural state, early painted pieces are not uncommon. Itinerant twig craftsmen often decorated their work with dots and dashes of paint, probably trying to add drama to what was considered to be a plain piece. With the variety of quick-drying paints currently available, we are afforded greater leeway to add color and the freedom to change it on a whim. Painted twig furniture can range from sophisticated to naive. Rainbow bands or random dots of color will set a mood and create a style.

Color Suggestions
Twig pieces spray-painted white and combined with white wicker—on a sun porch, in a child's room, or in a breakfast room—create a light, breezy feeling. A single large piece painted shiny black or dark green, such as a chaise or loveseat, can add drama to a traditional setting.

For a touch of whimsy, try using unexpected hues, such as Chinese red, teal blue, or lavender. The wide-ranging decorating styles so popular today allow you to create an effect that is all your own. You might even want to try a combination of colors on one piece. Try borrowing ideas for unique color combinations from other works, such as an Amish quilt, a favorite fabric, or a cherished piece of needlepoint. Experiment with the different available paints—artist's acrylic paints offer the most varied assortment of hues and can be made shiny or left flat, depending on the overcoat used as a sealer. Latex wall paint is good to cover large pieces and can be used as a first coat under acrylic.

CHAPTER 2

Finding the Wood

Rustic furniture designs are dictated by the character of the wood they are made from, so it is important to be able to identify various trees and shrubs and to familiarize yourself with their individual characteristics. Since not all trees are available in all regions or climates, I want to encourage you to experiment with your local materials. You will also want to learn various cultivating techniques to avoid destroying existing stands so they are preserved for future generations.

For the purposes of this book, you should know that trees are single-stemmed plants that attain a height of at least 15 feet, while shrubs are often multi-stemmed and generally grow to about 10 feet. Twigs are young limbs, called shoots when they are new growth, and are usually not more than two inches in diameter. Learning to recognize species under various growing conditions is not always easy. Many trees that grow at high elevations on mountains are twisted and sprawling as a result of a short growing season and strong winds, while at low levels they will be tall and straight. When searching for wood, you should carry a tree identification manual to help you recognize trees by their leaves, flowers, fruits, and bark.

A very good manual for tree identification is the series by the Nature Study Guild, Box 972, Berkeley, Calif., 94701. Send for their catalog for your area, such as *Pacific Coast Tree Finder, Rocky Mountain Tree Finder, Desert Tree Finder,* or *Winter Tree Finder.* These are small manuals that can be kept in your pocket or in the glove compartment of your car. Other helpful manuals are: *The Simon and*

Schuster Pocket Guide to Trees; Trees and Shrubs (Northeastern and Central North America); and *The Peterson Field Guide Series.*

COLLECTING TWIGS AND BRANCHES

If you do not own your own "back 40" country acres where you can gather twigs and limbs, here are some lessons in creative harvesting. One woman who lives in a small city told me she befriended the park workers in the city park. As they prune trees, they save some of the longer branches for her. She rewards them at holidays with homemade pies, and now has several examples of chairs and baskets in her apartment. I do not want to tell you to wish for a calamity, but a friend of mine in Iowa recently experienced a dreadful ice storm, with tree branches breaking off under the weight of the ice. While his neighbors were bemoaning the loss of favorite trees, he was busy gathering twigs for future projects. Be alert for innovative ways to secure your materials. Fruit orchards, such as apple, pear, or cherry, can be another good source of materials. Search out sites where developers and builders are working in your area. All too often such commercial ventures will destroy precious natural resources. Although this is heartbreaking, you can put the cut trees to good use, rather than seeing them wasted in a burning pit. I have even heard about someone who approached a builder to obtain some cut trees, and was offered pay to cart them away. Now there is an agreeable situation! Friendly farmers or loggers might be glad to sell you a small amount of twigs and limbs for a nominal charge. There are many innovative ways to obtain materials, and if you are enterprising I know you will succeed.

How to Choose and Gather Twigs
Always select fresh materials. Cut the twigs with care and be sure you don't pull the roots out. If you are collecting thin branches, such as willow, leave more than you remove, so that you preserve the plant and are assured a plentiful future supply. Use only sharp cutting tools (axes, saws, or clippers), and never rip or tear the branches, as this can destroy a living plant. Examine the twigs for insects or larvae, and try to avoid any pests. If these seem to be a problem, treat the wood with a safe garden insecticide before building your furniture.

How to Examine the Twigs for Larvae
When you are gathering twigs and poles, take time to check for insect activity, since you will not want to build furniture out of infested wood. Wood-eating insects on

living trees are relatively rare. Most wood eaters feed on dead trees. If your cut wood supply is kept outside for a prolonged period, it will become a target for bugs. Examine the branches for tiny holes or deep channels. This is not necessarily a sure-fire method for detecting live insects, but it is a clue for further investigation. If you suspect that a branch is infested, separate it from the rest of your supply for a week, and check it daily. If you find small piles of sawdust around or near the holes, the limb should be discarded.

Watch for twig-boring insects when you are harvesting thin twigs and vines. The larvae of beetles often bore through tender twigs and small branches, killing large portions of a tree's crown. When you are out collecting twigs, remember to look up. Learn to recognize the signs of tree damage.

If you find signs of insect activity after your piece is built, you will have to spray with an insecticide. Several safe, effective insecticides are available today, and more are being developed. Check with your local nursery or hardware store, and make sure the product you use is safe for indoor use. While you should use a product that is made with a natural *botanical pyrethrin* base, depending on the percentage of pyrethins it contains, it may be inappropriate for inside use. Be sure to read the label carefully. It is always best to apply the insecticide outdoors.

ALDER

Eight species of native alder grow rapidly in North America, often forming thickets in moist soil. All alder trees have irregularly toothed, prominently veined, oval or oblong leaves. The red alder tree of the Pacific Northwest often reaches heights of 30 to 40 feet, and the outside edges of its leaves are rolled under. The white alder, although usually smaller, is similar to the red alder, except that its leaves are flat. The Sitka alder is distinctive because of its smooth grey-green bark, covered with warty clusters. The undersides of its outermost leaves are glossy and sticky. The thin leaf alder and the mountain alder have oblong leaves, two to three inches wide, with orange-brown midribs that sport rusty brown hairs. The undersides of its leaves are dull, not sticky. The Arizona alder, which grows in the southwestern United States, has slightly smaller leaves with a yellow midrib and a smooth, grey to brownish bark. The seaside alder, on the other hand, grows on the east coast. With its round-topped crown of zigzag branches, it is quite easy to identify.

The alder is a relatively obscure tree, and it is often overlooked as a viable wood for twig furnishings. However, as a close cousin to birch and hazelnut, its pliable branches are invaluable. Alder can be used to make basket handles, and to form the arched backs on chairs. Larger pieces can be used as chair supports, and for tables and plant stands.

Where Alder Trees Grow
Most alder grows in the western regions of the United States and Canada. It is easily distinguishable in the spring, when staminate catkins cast a distinctive greenish-brown hue over the surrounding area. Alder is found around lakes, along streams and creek beds, and in open swamps.

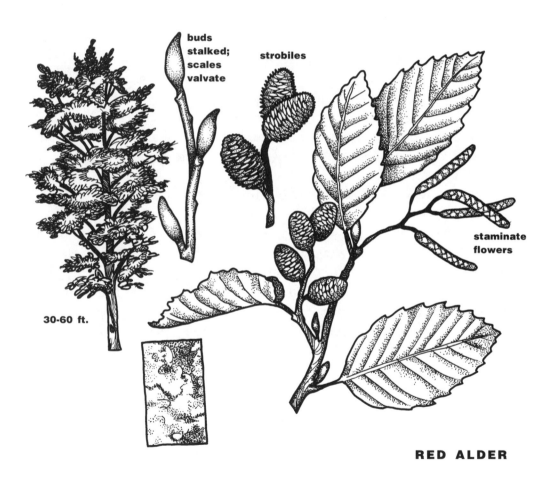

buds
stalked;
scales
valvate

strobiles

staminate
flowers

30-60 ft.

RED ALDER

BEECH

There are almost 100 species of beech native to North America. They are handsome, deciduous trees with short-stemmed, prominently veined, elliptical leaves, three to six inches long. Their smooth bark is blue-grey and commonly blotched with dark grey speckling and thin split lines. On older beech trees a smoky, dark tone is often noticeable on one side of the trunk, with still darker areas around the base. Young beech trees are easily recognizable by their deep red-brown buds, covered with cream-colored flecks.

Beech wood is tight-grained, heavy, and strong. Because the bark on beech trees is strong and tight, it does not peel off easily, making it particularly desirable for making twig chairs and tables.

Where Beech Trees Grow
Beech trees are usually found in deep forests, surrounded by oaks or maples. They grow from Southern Ontario to Nova Scotia, from Central Wisconsin to Maine, and south to Texas and Northern Florida.

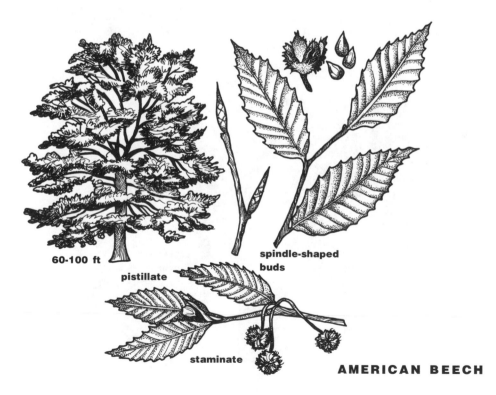

60-100 ft

spindle-shaped
buds

pistillate

staminate

AMERICAN BEECH

BIRCH

While you'll find information on white paper birch in the "Barks and Vines" chapter, there are many other useful birches growing throughout most of North America. One of them is the low-growing Alaskan shrub called ground birch, which is an important summer food for northern animals. Yellow birch yields bark that is yellowish to bronze, which peels into thin, narrow strips. Water birch is a small, slender tree, often with drooping branches and a dark brown bark. River birch has a scaly, grey-black trunk on older trees, and thin, pinkish bark on young trees. The river birch's trunk is often divided into multi-arched limbs, while the blueleaf birch grows most commonly as a shrub, with a rosy-hued bark that does not peel. Yukon birch is a stately tree that often reaches heights of 25 feet. It can be identified by its dark brown bark and white lenticel clusters (ventilating pores in the bark). Black birch is set apart from the other birches with its mahogany-red bark, smooth and glossy in young trees, and rough and scaly in older trees. Its leaves and bark have a sweet, minty aroma, and it is sometimes called sweet birch. Birch leaves vary in shape, but all have prominent veins and short leaf stems.

The strength of birch and the coloring of its bark make it very desirable for building twig furniture. Its sturdy limbs are useful for making chairs, tables, and shelves.

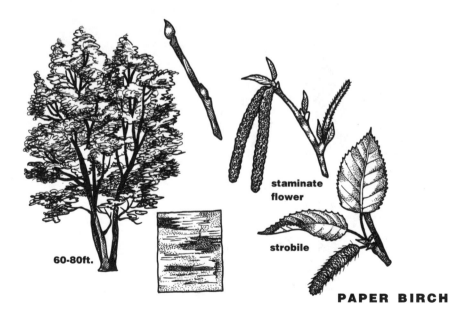

60-80ft.

staminate flower

strobile

PAPER BIRCH

Where Birch Trees Grow

Birch trees grow rapidly, often forming extensive forests in the north. Yellow and black birch grow along the east coast, from northern Canada into the United States as far south as Georgia. Water birch and Yukon birch grow in the western United States and Canada. River birch is the only native birch that grows at low elevations, along streams in the southeastern United States. Blueleaf birch is found in Maine and eastern Quebec, along the St. Lawrence River valley. Its blue-green leaves make it easy to identify.

BOX ELDER

The box elder has three-leaflet leaves with jagged edges, similar to maple leaves in shape. Its bark is pastel red, purple, or bright green, often coated with a thin white haze. Box elder branches are brittle when dry, so it may be helpful to soak them in a bucket of water until ready for use. These colorful and glossy twigs are suitable for small projects such as picture frames.

Where Box Elder Trees Grow

Box elder grows in the western United States, from Illinois to Colorado and northern Texas up to the Pacific Northwest. It is an extremely adaptable tree, growing on high or low ground, in sunlight or shade, in moist or dry areas.

50-70 ft.

BOX ELDER

CEDAR

Most cedar wood is aromatic, including some cypress and juniper. Cedar foliage is compact and dark with a slightly prickly texture. Incense cedars are covered with dark brown, deeply furrowed bark. Northern white cedar and Atlantic white cedar also have deeply furrowed barks, ranging in color from ash-grey to reddish-brown. Western red cedar is distinguishable by its vertically ridged, brownish-grey, shredded bark. Port Orford cedar has dark green foliage similar to the Western red cedar's, but the scales on its branches are tighter. Alaska cedar is a smaller tree with yellow-green foliage and a rougher texture than the Port Orford. It usually has grey shaggy bark and thin scales. Its interior wood is most often yellow in appearance.

Sturdy cedar limbs are useful as table legs with simple board tops. Their shaggy bark adds texture and interest to any project. Cedar poles are especially useful where strong supports are required.

Where Cedar Trees Grow

Cedar in one form or another is plentiful throughout most of the United States and Canada. It is found alongside water bodies from North Dakota to Maine and southern Ontario, and then south to central Texas and northern Florida. In the northwest, throughout Oregon, Washington, and British Columbia, cedars of various types grow in abundance. Its shaggy bark, remarkable shape, and unique aroma make it easy to locate.

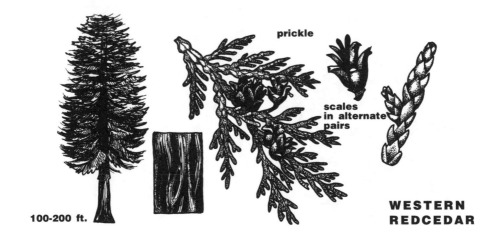

100-200 ft.

prickle

scales in alternate pairs

WESTERN REDCEDAR

CHERRY

Cherry trees grow in abundance throughout most parts of the northern hemisphere, often in cool regions. Black cherry is usually easy to identify because of its distinctive color. In the sapling stage, its bark is smooth and reddish-brown, turning dark grey and flaky on mature trees. All cherry trees have simple, alternating leaves that are two to five inches long, a bit leathery, and serrated along their edges.

The strength and beautiful coloring of the young cherry saplings make them ideal for twig chair parts as well as for tables. The wood is usually free from warping, but should be well-seasoned before it is used because it shrinks during seasoning.

Where Cherry Trees Grow
Cherry trees of one type or another are common throughout most of North America. The black cherry grows in rich soils and woods from southeastern Manitoba to Nova Scotia, and from eastern South Dakota to Maine and south to eastern Texas and central Florida.

The pin cherry grows 15 to 25 feet tall, and is found across most of Canada to Nova Scotia, and as far south as South Carolina to the east and Utah in the west.

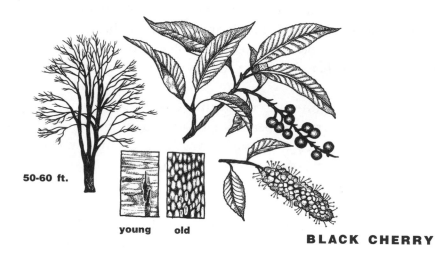

50-60 ft.

young   old

BLACK CHERRY

The common chokecherry is a shrub or small tree found in most of North America, except in the extreme southern areas of Texas, Arkansas, Louisiana, Alabama, Georgia, and Florida. It can grow 25 feet tall and up to eight inches in diameter. The chokecherry has white flowers in the spring, and tiny, dark red cherries in the summer, usually about one-third of an inch in diameter.

The bitter cherry has red to black cherries, about half an inch in diameter. Distinguishable by its brownish bark with horizontal, orange lenticels, it can grow to 40 feet and 18 inches in diameter. The bitter cherry occurs along the western half of North America—from British Columbia and Alberta throughout most of Washington and Oregon—and as far east and south as parts of Nevada and Arizona.

Hollyleaf cherry has egg-shaped, evergreen leaves, one to two inches long and an inch wide. Along with the rare Catalina cherry, it grows along the extreme western coast of California.

BALD CYPRESS

The bald cypress, also known as southern or red cypress, can grow to grand heights of 100 feet. It has yellow-green needles that turn brown before falling in the autumn. Bald cypress also produces wrinkled cones about an inch wide that mature in one season. Its branches are often draped with Spanish moss.

Bald cypress forms "knees," which are really branches that grow out of its widespread underground root system. These sharp, pointed extensions project above the surface. Craftspeople often use these "knees" to create lamp bases and sculptures.

Bald cypress is most often used to build Gypsy-style chairs, loveseats, and planters. Its naturally pale bark is beautiful left in its natural state, and looks lovely indoors or on covered porches. Cypress will weather to a soft grey. Left outside for a season, your weathered cypress piece will be appreciated for its subtle coloring.

Where Cypress Trees Grow
The bald cypress is probably familiar to those who live along the southern part of the United States. It grows in large forests, especially in the wet coastal plains of Florida. Although not all bald cypress grows in water, it is abundant where periodic flooding is common. Most often associated with rustic work from Florida, the species has a large growing area, ranging from southern New Jersey to Florida, along the Atlantic Coastal Plain, across the Gulf Coast Lowlands into Texas and Mexico, and up the Mississippi basin as far as Illinois and Indiana.

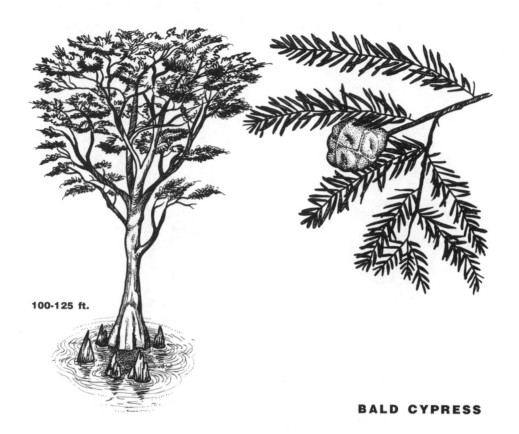

BALD CYPRESS

EUCALYPTUS (BLUE GUM)

Eucalyptus bark is usually thin and reddish-brown in color. It peels off in long strips, revealing a creamy-white or grey underbark. Its leathery curved leaves are pale green, six to 12 inches long, with a sharp tip. The blue gum can grow to heights of 200 feet.

Eucalyptus benefits from frequent pruning, and 10-year-old trees can provide a continuous supply of branches useful for picture frames, chair parts, and a variety of other twig projects.

Where Eucalyptus Trees Grow

The branches and bark of over 200 species of Australian eucalyptus trees are widely used in constructing twig furniture. In North America, the blue gum eucalyptus is generally found on the western border of California, south to Arizona and New

Mexico, stretching along the Gulf Coast of Texas, and east to Florida. Because of its capacity to grow in semi-arid regions, blue gum eucalyptus has been widely planted for windbreaks along dry fields.

50-100 ft. flowers

nut

bur

**GOLDEN
CHINKAPIN**

GOLDEN CHINKAPIN
(GOLDEN LEAF CHESTNUT)

The golden chinkapin has leathery, oblong, evergreen leaves, two to five inches long, with smooth curled margins. Its flowers and burrs resemble those of chestnuts, but are smaller. On young trees the bark is smooth, and on older trees, it is broken into reddish-brown ridges.

The twigs and branches from young trees are useful for making table legs, chair supports, and plant stands.

Where Golden Chinkapin Trees Grow
Golden chinkapins cluster along the western coast of North America from northern California to southern Oregon along the edges of pine and hemlock stands.

HAZEL

Small trees or shrubs, hazel reaches heights of three to six feet. Its leaves are hairy, oval or elliptical, and have a heart-shaped base and coarse, double-toothed margins. In the spring, the hazel's staminate catkins resemble those of birch, but its buds are oval and its fruit is a tiny nut enclosed by a leafy husk. In autumn, the leaves of the American hazel turn dull yellow, while the leaves of the beaked hazel (hazelnut) become bright yellow. Hazel twigs are dark brown, ranging from smooth on American hazel to rough on beaked hazel.

Hazel shoots are strong and its bark—which ranges from reddish-brown to yellowish-brown—is often densely hairy, lending a unique velvet appearance to twig projects. Supple young branches are useful for fashioning baskets, while older branches make sturdy chair and table supports.

Where Hazel Trees Grow
American hazel occurs from Maine and Ontario south to Florida and Kansas. The beaked hazel tree grows from Nova Scotia to British Columbia, south to Georgia and Tennessee, and west from Kansas to Oregon. It grows in thickets, in moist or dry conditions and light soil, at the edge of woods or beside walls.

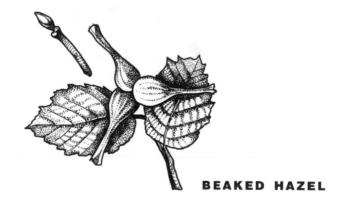

BEAKED HAZEL

WITCH HAZEL

Witch hazel can be identified by its odd yellow flowers, which consist of four twisting petals, each about three-quarters of an inch long. The flowers appear in autumn and continue to hang on the bare branches after the leaves have fallen.

Witch hazel is most often used for small projects, such as baskets, magazine racks, and plant stands.

Where Witch Hazel Trees Grow
Witch hazel is a small tree or shrub that grows in shady ground, and in the undergrowth of forests throughout the eastern half of the United States and Canada and as far south as Texas.

WITCH-HAZEL

HICKORY

Hickory has often been called the most durable of native American hardwoods. In fact, when twig furniture manufacturing became a commercial venture in 1899, the Old Hickory Furniture Company chose hickory as its sole wood, and even today continues to manufacture hickory furniture in the traditional manner. Hickory is most commonly used for joined furniture (with a mortise and tenon structure) as opposed to my nailed-together designs, which are much easier for the novice.

Hickory bark is usually smooth and grey when young, becoming irregular with age. Its frayed edges give it a shaggy appearance. There are 11 hickories native to North America that can be used for twig furniture. The shagbark hickory has a distinctive, shaggy bark composed of thin, narrow scales that curve outward at the ends. Shellbark hickory resembles shagbark, but its leaves are very long, from 15 to 20 inches. Mockernut hickory has fragrant leaves that are eight to 13 inches long, with hairy stalks and narrow leaflets. Pignut hickory has a scaly bark that forms diamond-shaped ridges on mature trees, while bitternut hickory is distinguished from pignut by its smooth, grey bark. Water hickory produces leaves with reddish, hairy stems. Black hickory is easily recognizable because of its deeply furrowed black bark and its dark, reddish-brown nut. Nutmeg hickory's bark is scaly and reddish-brown, and its dark green leaves are often silvery-white on their lower surfaces.

SHELLBARK HICKORY

Hickory saplings can be grown in a coppice, which is a woodland planted to yield a continuous harvest of twigs.

Where Hickory Trees Grow
Shagbark, shellbark, and black hickories grow on low hillsides and river bottoms, while pignut, mockernut, bitternut, and nutmeg grow in dry highlands. Water hickory is found along river swamps from southeastern Virginia to Florida and west to Texas. Most hickories grow throughout eastern and central North America.

CALIFORNIA LAUREL (OREGON MYRTLE)

California laurel has leaves that resemble the eastern mountain laurel, but they are broader ovals and smell like bay rum. It has a greenish-brown bark, either smooth or scaly, and is most often considered a shrub rather than a tree. California laurel is very hard when dry, and so is superb for building sturdy furniture. Its gnarled, twisted limbs make interesting chair supports and magazine stands.

Where California Laurel (Oregon Myrtle) Trees Grow
California laurel grows along the extreme west coast in Oregon and California.

MADRONE (ARBUTUS)

This branch of the heath family is made up of more than 1,500 species growing in acid soils. Most are shrubs, and all have simple and—in most varieties—alternating leaves. Blueberries, rhododendrons, and heathers are familiar varieties of the heath family. Madrone can be easily recognized because of its thin, red-brown bark. Its wood is soft, and becomes hard and brittle when dry. Limbs two inches in diameter are useful for making chairs and tables, but smaller twigs should be soaked in a bucket of water and stored in a cool place until they are ready for use (usually within a week). Madrone's beautiful bark, often the color of terra cotta with green patches, makes unique picture frames and baskets.

Where Madrone (Arbutus) Trees Grow
The Pacific madrone grows along the northwestern coast, from British Columbia to as far south as San Diego, Calif. Texas and Arizona madrone trees grow in their respective regions, and are quite similar in appearance to the northern ones. Sour-

wood is a variety that occurs in Louisiana, Georgia, Tennessee, and the Carolinas. Lyonia grows throughout Florida and has a reddish-brown, usually scaly, bark that forms ridges on a twisted trunk.

50-100 ft.

PACIFIC MADRONE

MULBERRY

Mulberry belongs to a family that includes osage orange, commonly used for making archery bows. Two herbs, hop and hemp, are also included in the mulberry family. The three species most commonly used for building rustic furniture are red mulberry, Texas mulberry, and osage orange. Red mulberry produces deciduous leaves that are three to five inches long and two to three inches wide. It grows to heights of 60 feet, and its leaves turn yellow in the fall. Texas mulberry is similar but smaller, growing to only 15 feet in height. Its leaves are usually only an inch long. Osage orange produces multi-veined, deciduous leaves between three and five inches long, which turn bright yellow in autumn. Often used for hedge plantings, orange osage is distinctive because of its thorny twigs.

Mulberry twigs are useful for many small projects, such as making picture frames or small baskets. Close-grained osage orange is hard and strong, and once its thorns are clipped, it is useful for almost all rustic projects.

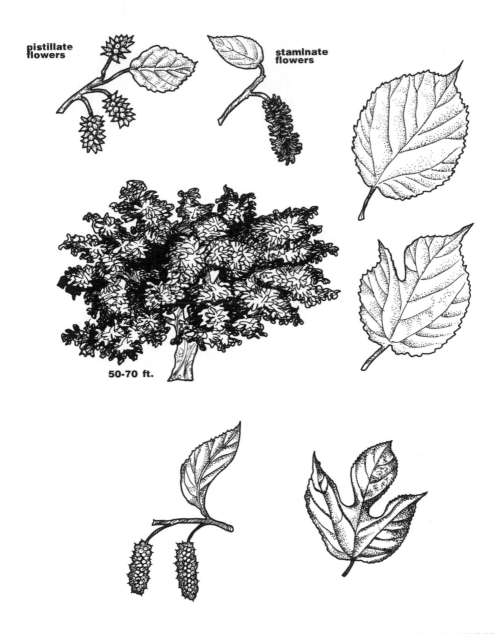

pistillate flowers

staminate flowers

50-70 ft.

RED MULBERRY

Where Mulberry Trees Grow

Red mulberry grows in rich woodlands throughout Ontario, New York, and Vermont, from Minnesota to South Dakota, and from Florida to Texas. Texas mulberry, as its name implies, occurs as a small tree or shrub throughout the state and in the arid southwestern areas of North America. Osage orange can be found throughout most of the south and central portions of North America. It can be easily identified by its greenish-yellow bark and rough, inedible fruit, which ranges from three to five inches in diameter.

SWEETGUM

In the summer, sweetgum can be identified by its five-lobed, star-shaped, aromatic leaves. During autumn, these bright green leaves turn a brilliant red and gold. Its fruit is easily recognizable by its long stem and woody, burl-like head about one-and-a-half inches in diameter. The sweetgum's bark is scored with grey to brown ridges.

Where Sweetgum Trees Grow

Sweetgum grows in wet soils from southwestern Connecticut and southern New York to southern Missouri and eastern Texas. It is found as far south as central Florida.

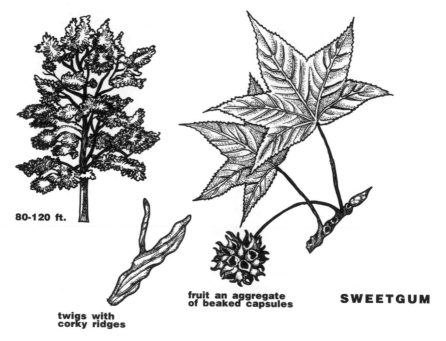

80-120 ft.

twigs with
corky ridges

fruit an aggregate
of beaked capsules

SWEETGUM

PACIFIC DOGWOOD

The leaves of Pacific dogwood resemble those of flowering dogwood but are larger, about four to six inches long and two to three inches wide. Its bark ranges from dark brown to black and is usually smooth, with scaly plates clustered around the bases of large trees. Pacific dogwood's showy white petals usually number six instead of the four found on the eastern dogwood.

Twigs and branches of Pacific dogwood can be substituted for beech or any other eastern hardwood when you are making chairs, tables, or picture frames.

Where Pacific Dogwood Trees Grow
Pacific dogwood grows at low elevations in shaded, coastal areas of western North America from British Columbia to San Francisco.

winter twig with flower bud

fruit

PACIFIC DOGWOOD

WILLOW

Last but not least, willow is the most important wood for making rustic twig furniture. Luckily, the tree (shrub) grows throughout most of North America, and there are more than 100 rapidly growing species in the northern hemisphere. Because willow hybridizes in nature, true identification is often impossible, but it is also not necessary for our purposes.

All willows have long, thin leaves that are slightly notched, and catkins with varying amounts of silky fuzz. Early spring pussy willows can be found along frozen rivers in many areas, where a few branches may be gathered and brought into a warm house to "force" the sight of spring. Pussy willows can also be found standing in bunches at city florist shops at a time when the snow has become a grimy March blanket. (Purchased willows can often be used for small projects such as miniature chairs.)

All willow is pliable when green, and its flexible twigs create the warped, sculpted style of most rustic twig furniture. Its strength and flexibility are invaluable for making basket handles, loveseats, chairs, chaise lounges, and baby cradles. Willow has a long history—the North American Indians used young willow shoots to fashion baskets, fish traps, and cradle carriers. Willow shoots usually remain flexible for up to two weeks after harvesting, but it is a good idea to soak the shoots in a bucket of water in a cool place until you are ready to use them. Permit yourself a few tries at bending them before beginning your project. Do not rush the bending and arching—slow and steady is the key here. With a little practice the novice can soon become an expert.

PACIFIC WILLOW

Where Willow Trees Grow
Willow usually grows along streams and creek beds, and in places where the soil is moist. Because most types of willow are similar, it is not necessary to identify each species. However, for those of you out on a willow-hunt in various parts of the country, I would like to mention some of the North American willows. In the western portions of the United States there are the Pacific willow, feltleaf willow,

scouler willow, and hooker willow. The peachleaf willow grows throughout the south-central portion of the United States, as do the sandbar willow and the yewleaf willow. Balsam willow, bog willow, sage willow, and pussy willow are the most common willows of eastern North America. Diamond willow and hoary willow grow throughout most of North America in bogs and lowlands. Some of the finest willow in the world comes from areas where long growing seasons, cool nights, sunny days, and rich damp soil create ideal growing conditions for long straight shoots.

Willow roots easily, and is often planted in coppices. The most common, fast-growing tree, willow provides shoots during its first year that are excellent for making baskets, and a full twig crop suitable for making furniture during its third and fourth year. To plant willow for future harvesting, cut 12-inch lengths of willow shoots and plant them 10 inches deep, 18 inches apart in rich soil, preferably along a creek bed. In three to four years, a good willow crop for making twig furniture will be ready to harvest. Willow requires pruning to permit young shoots to grow; it is nature's way of recycling!

Peeled Willow

While bark is left on for almost all twig pieces, some craftspeople are experimenting with peeled willow work. It is usually best to peel the willow in the spring and summer months when the trees are growing and the cells beneath the bark are dividing rapidly. Cut the willow poles before peeling. Using a sharp knife, score a line down the length of the pole through the bark, and the "skin" should slip off. If not, carefully pry the bark loose with your fingers. Smooth, barkless willow, the color of a Kansas wheat field, has the look of natural wicker.

CHAPTER 3

Basic Methods for Working with Twigs

The first requirement, of course, is wood. Chapter 2, Finding the Wood, will tell you how to locate raw materials in your area. Try to find branches with interesting markings and unusual shapes, as they will help inspire your imagination and add uniqueness to your finished work.

Although most books on the subject suggest that wood should be cut in the winter to preserve the bark, I have not found this to be true, and have cut twigs in the spring and fall that have retained their bark as well. If, however, you want to strip the bark, cut in the summer when the trees are growing and the cells between the bark and the wood are dividing.

TOOLS AND EQUIPMENT

You will need the following tools and equipment to build your twig furniture:

A crosscut hand saw, coping saw, single bit axe, garden shears, and/or clippers will be necessary for gathering the twigs.

A ⅜-inch variable-speed drill (electric or cordless is best—using an old-fashioned hand drill will take a little longer to finish your project) with a selection of bits; a hammer; and galvanized flathead nails in #4p, #6p, #8p, #10p, #12p, and #16p sizes are required to assemble the pieces of your project. You will also need a marking pencil, measuring tape or ruler, safety glasses, and work gloves. (Always use safety glasses or goggles when working with wood to shield your face and eyes from flying wood chips and sawdust.)

Optional Tools and Supplies

You may also need some of the following:

- For finer projects, ¾-inch finishing nails.
- A crosscut saw or key-hole saw.
- A cordless drill or hand drill for working on location.
- A ⅜-inch reversible drill if available.
- A drift punch (10 to 12 inches long) or a pocket knife for some projects.
- For the baskets and cube, 12-gauge wire and a wood chisel, and a two-inch rubber mallet for the frames.
- Linseed oil and turpentine or polyurethane if a piece is to be used out-of-doors for prolonged periods of time. A spray bottle or electric airless sprayer for applying the linseed oil/turpentine mixture.

CHOOSING AND STORING BRANCHES

Always gather more branches than are required. Some of the lengths, diameters, and shapes you choose in the woods will not be suitable for the particular piece you are planning to build. It is a good idea to have a supply on hand.

Always gather more willow or other pliable branches than you need. It is not unusual to break a few during bending, especially when you are first getting started.

After each piece is cut, identify the part with a small slip of paper taped to the branch. This will help you quickly identify each branch as you assemble the project.

Fresh, green branches are suitable for all projects. Seasoned (dry) branches are suitable when bending is not required, especially for making chair and table legs. Only green branches can be used for the bendable parts. For best results, use fresh willow or vines within a few days of cutting. If this is not possible, stand the willow twigs in a bucket of water, placed where they cannot freeze. They can last for several weeks if you remember to keep the bucket filled with water. In order to keep vines supple, coil them into a wreath shape and submerge in a bucket of water with rocks placed on top of them to weigh the coil down.

BUILDING THE PROJECT

After the wood has been gathered and the pieces selected and cut to size, assemble the basic frame structure, following the directions given. When the sub-assemblies are complete, it often helps to have someone hold the pieces upright while you connect the two sub-assemblies. The basic frame is then ready for the addition of the other pieces, such as arms, backs, and seats. The bent willow is generally applied last. Here again it is a good idea to enlist an assistant to bend the willow (or alder) and hold it in place while you drill the pilot holes and nail the pieces together.

Checking for Strength and Safety

When your project is complete, check the stretchers, rails, and all other connecting beams for strength. This is especially important for chairs and tables. Turn your finished piece over, and try to move the connecting members to ensure that the joints are secure. The joints should not wobble or move. At this point, if there is play in the joints, you may have to add extra nails, being sure to drill pilot holes first.

About Nails

Flathead galvanized nails are used for most of the joinery. Their subtle grey coloring blends in nicely with most wood tones, while their broad, flat heads ensure a firm joint. Galvanized nails do not rust and their rough surfaces hold well in both green and seasoned wood.

Finishing nails with small heads (sometimes called panel nails) are used for attaching thin twigs, usually the decorative elements.

Nails are sized in terms of pennies (#p), originally signifying the price per hundred. A #2p nail is one inch long, a #4p is one-and-a-half inches long, a #6p is two inches long, and so on.

Keep an assortment of galvanized nails near your work area. When you select a nail for each joint, make sure that it is just a little shorter than the combined thickness of the two twigs you are joining. The drill bit you use should be slightly smaller in diameter than the nail you plan to use. Drill each hole to a depth that is three-quarters of the length of the nail. You want the nail to bite firmly into the second member of the joint.

Use branches as braces for strength and rigidity. Add the braces front-to-back and side-to-side to keep the piece from swaying. They should form a triangle with two of the perpendicular branches of the piece—for example, leg and cross beams, or leg and side rails. When selecting branches for braces, remember that forked pieces are decorative while still being functional.

The bent back of a loveseat or chaise is assembled by attaching and bending the back hoops one at a time until you have three or four running sequentially. Bend and attach the spokes next, inserting them between the hoops to secure them. After all the spokes have been inserted, wrap and weave the back with flexible willow, alder, or lengths of vine. Be sure to keep this final wrapping tight in order to stabilize the spokes. (Optional: Use finishing nails here to secure the wrapping.)

After the piece is completely assembled, it is a good practice to inspect all the joints and add nails where necessary to strengthen the assembly. An additional nail is usually required where a beam, a rail, and a leg meet, so that three nails are used at the joint.

Pilot Holes

Drilling holes before nailing (called pilot holes) will keep the wood from splitting as it dries. Select a bit that is slightly smaller in diameter than the thickness of the nail you are using. Pilot holes should be snug and shorter than the nail by about three-eighths of an inch.

Butt Construction

When project directions call for butt construction, it simply means that the end of one member fits flush against the other to form the joint.

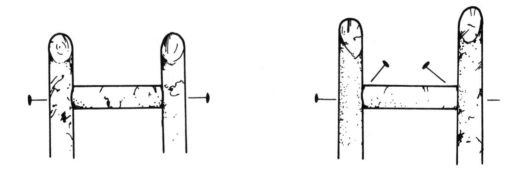

Lap Construction

In this procedure, two pieces are notched so that they can fit tightly together. This will form a double layer with the same thickness as one whole piece. Make sure the notches are large enough so they don't put stress on the joint but tight enough so there is no play. For our purposes, lap construction is used when making picture frames.

Overlap Construction

In overlap construction, one member extends over an adjoining piece to form the joint. This technique is usually used on front and back seat supports, and on chair stretchers.

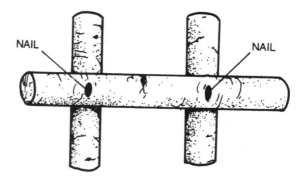

CHAPTER 4

Twig Furniture

L OVESEAT

This four-and-a-half-foot long and four-foot high loveseat is a cozy addition to any room. If you carefully choose the fabric for the cushion and pillows, its graceful curves will blend in with any surroundings.

MATERIALS

Willow, alder, or any pliable branches ranging from 52" to 125" in length and from ½" to 1" in diameter may be used for the arched back and seat supports. You will also need at least two forked pliable branches. A selection of very supple branches, as long as possible and ¼" to ½" in diameter, will be needed for wrapping the arched back. (Note: Four lengths of local vine—such as wisteria or honeysuckle—54" long and ¾" in diameter, can be substituted for wrapping the arched back.) Hardwoods such as beech, birch, or cherry will also be needed, in lengths from 21" to 55" and in diameters from ¾" to 2". You will also need galvanized flathead nails in assorted sizes (#4p, #6p, #8p, #12p, and #16p) and about 24 ¾" finishing nails. Linseed oil and turpentine will be needed if the piece is to be used outdoors.

TOOLS

- ◆ Crosscut hand saw
- ◆ Single bit axe for felling trees
- ◆ ⅜" variable-speed drill
- ◆ Measuring tape
- ◆ Hammer
- ◆ Marking pencil

- ◆ Safety goggles
- ◆ Crosscut skill saw (optional)
- ◆ Keyhole saw (optional)
- ◆ Drift punch (optional)
- ◆ Pocket knife (optional)

LOVESEAT CUTTING CHART

NAME OF PART	QUANTITY	DIAMETER (INCHES)	LENGTH (INCHES)	DESCRIPTION
Legs A	4	2	21	hardwood
Front and lower beams B	3	1¼	50	hardwood
Back seat support beam BB	1	2	55	hardwood
Side beams C	4	1½	21	hardwood
Arms D	2	1¾	25	hardwood, curved
Upper back support beam B1	1	1½	55	hardwood, curved
Arched back F	4	½–1	125(10' 5")	pliable
Seat supports E	7	¾–1	52	pliable
Seat supports E	2	¾–1	52	forked, pliable
Seat rim G	1	¾	44	hardwood
Bottom brace X	1	¾	50	hardwood forked if possible
Side braces	2	¾	24	hardwood

NAME OF PART	QUANTITY	DIAMETER (INCHES)	LENGTH (INCHES)	DESCRIPTION
Wrap branches	selection	¼–½	as long as possible	very supple
Wrap vines	4	¾	54	very supple

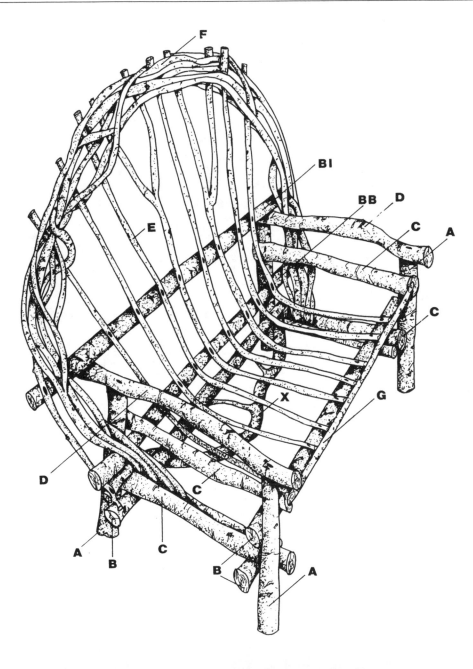

DIRECTIONS

Cutting the Branches

1. Cut four 2" diameter branches for legs A, each 21" long.
2. Cut three 1¼" diameter branches for front and lower beams B, each 50" long.
3. Cut one 2" diameter branch for back seat support beam BB, 55" long.
4. Cut four 1½" diameter branches for side beams C, 21" long.
5. Cut two 1¾" diameter branches for arms D, 25" long (curved branches make comfortable armrests).
6. Cut one 1½" diameter branch for upper back support beam B1, 55" long.
7. Cut four ½" to 1" diameter pliable willow or alder branches, each 125" long, to form arched back F.
8. Cut nine ¾" to 1" diameter willow, alder, or similar wood seat supports E, 52" long (try to include two forked branches).
9. Cut one ¾" diameter twig seat rim G, 44" long.
10. Cut one ¾" diameter bottom brace X (forked if possible), 50" long.
11. Cut two ¾" diameter side braces XX, 24" long.

Laying Out the Sub-Assembly

1. Drill pilot holes 7" from the ends of two beams B, and 3" up from the bottom of the four legs A on the inside. Beams B will extend approximately 3" beyond each leg A.
2. Join front and back bottom beams to the legs using a #12p nail. Nail from the inside.
3. Drill holes through the side ends of lower side beams C, and 6" up from the bottom of legs A. Nail in place from the inside using #12p nails.
4. Drill holes 6" from each end of back seat support beam BB, and 15" up from the bottom of back legs A.
5. Attach back support beam BB to back leg A from the inside, using a #12p nail.
6. Drill holes through the third upper front beam B into front legs A from the inside, 15" from the bottom of each leg, making it level with back seat support beam BB.
7. Nail in place from the inside using a #12p nail.
8. Place upper side beams C on top of upper front beam B and back seat support beam BB. Drill holes and nail in place.
9. Lay arms D on top of legs A. The arms should extend about 2" beyond the front and back of legs A. Make sure the back of arms D are long enough to support back support beam B1.

10. Drill holes through the arms and into the top of the legs at the point where they meet. Nail in place using #8p or #10p nails.
11. Lay back support beam B1 on top of arms D.

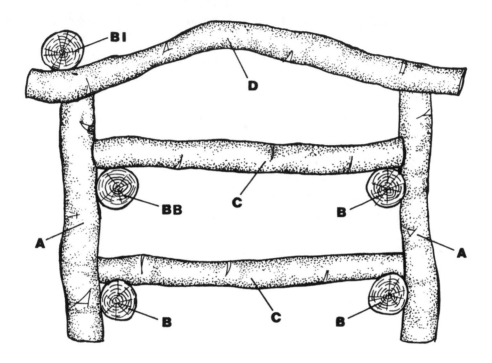

12. Drill holes through back support beam B1 and into the top of arms D at the point where they meet. Nail in place using #8p nails.

Fitting and Assembling the Arched Back
1. Select one back twig to be used in the arch and position it inside bottom side beam C, against lower back beam BB on the outside of upper side beam C, and finally, against back support beam B1.
2. Drill holes at the meeting points and nail in place.
3. Gently bend the twig into an arched shape and attach in the same manner to the opposite side.
4. Repeat steps 1 through 3 with two more back pieces F.
5. Position the remaining back twig F along the outside of back leg A, upward along the outside of lower back beam BB, and outside back support beam B1, nailing carefully into place.

6. Again, gently bend the twig into an arched shape, as in steps 3 and 4 above, and nail into place as in step 5.

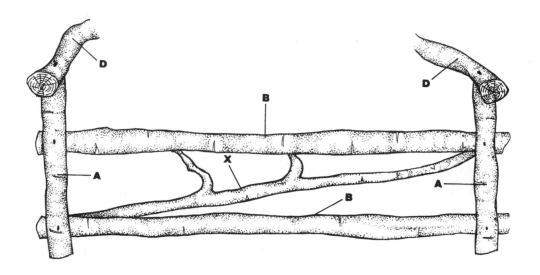

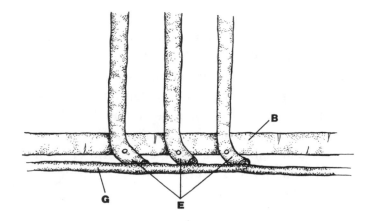

Attaching the Seat
1. Working from the center, position twig E along the top of the front beam B. Drill and nail in place using #6p nails. Gently bend upward toward seat support beam BB and back support beam B1. Drill and nail.
2. Insert the free end of E through the arched back bows F.
3. Repeat with eight remaining seat supports E, working from either side of the center twig outward.

Wrapping the Top

1. Wrap one end of a ¼" to ½" diameter pliable vine around the four arched seat back twigs near seat support beam BB. Weave it under and over the top of C, between the tops of seat supports E, into the arched branches, and tuck it in at the opposite side. Continue to wrap and weave two or three pliable vine branches into the arch to stabilize the back bows. Drill and nail in place where necessary.

2. To finish the seat, face the front of seat supports E with seat rim G. Join seat rim G to the front of each seat support E with a ¾" finishing nail.

Bracing and Completing

1. Place bottom brace X on top of lower side beam C and bottom back beam B at a diagonal. Drill and nail in place. This bottom brace strengthens and supports the structure. Any forks should extend upward as a decorative element.

2. Join side braces XX to the lower inside front legs and the upper inside back legs. Drill and nail in place from the inside for added stability.

Finishing

You will find that the unique character and coloring of the wood grows more beautiful as the piece ages, and will want to leave it natural. To enhance the color of the wood, rub with tung oil. With all the nooks and crannies involved in this large piece, I suggest using a sprayer if you want to paint it. If your wood is very dark and you desire a lighter look, try a wash of a pale color. To color-wash your furniture, make a mixture of one-quarter water-based paint to three-quarters water. Then, using a stubby paint brush, dab on the wash, one section at a time. Before the paint dries, quickly rub off the painted section with a cloth until the desired effect is achieved. When dry, finish with a rub of tung oil.

SETTEE

This three-foot, cozy settee is a larger version of the occasional chair. A pair of settees arranged by the fireplace creates an intimate seating area. When a pair of chairs is added, you'll have all the seating you need for a small room. Placed at one end of the bedroom, a settee can help in establishing a warm retreat. A major feature of any room is the choice in fabrics. Choose your cushions carefully to add decorating flair. Consider a crisp black and white check, a faded romantic chintz, or a vintage Oriental rug.

MATERIALS

You will need 14 to 15 pliable branches 35" to 96" in length with a diameter of ¾" and hardwood branches of 6" to 38" in length with a diameter of 1¼" to 2". You will also need galvanized flathead nails in assorted sizes (#4p, #6p, #8p, and #10p) and about 24 1" finishing nails.

TOOLS

- ◆ Single bit axe for felling trees
- ◆ Crosscut hand saw
- ◆ Clippers or garden shears
- ◆ Ruler or measuring tape
- ◆ Marking pencil
- ◆ ⅜" variable-speed drill
- ◆ Hammer
- ◆ Safety goggles
- ◆ Work gloves
- ◆ Crosscut skill saw (optional)
- ◆ Keyhole saw (optional)
- ◆ Pocket knife (optional)

SETTEE CUTTING CHART

NAME OF PART	QUANTITY	DIAMETER (INCHES)	LENGTH (INCHES)	DESCRIPTION
Legs A	4	1¾	20	hardwood
Arms AA	2	2	24	hardwood
Side beams B	4	1¼	14¾	hardwood
Front beams C	2	1½	34¾	hardwood
Back bottom beam CC	1	1½	33	hardwood
Back supports D	2	1¼	38	hardwood
Seat support E	1	1¼	36¾	hardwood
Braces F	2	1	22½	hardwood
Back G	2–3	¾	96(8')	pliable
Seat/back GG	11	¾	38	pliable
Seat rim H	1	¾	38	pliable

NAME OF PART	QUANTITY	DIAMETER (INCHES)	LENGTH (INCHES)	DESCRIPTION
Arm wrap HH	1	½	35	pliable split in half lengthwise
Front beam brace I	1	1½	6	hardwood

D I R E C T I O N S

Cutting the Branches
1. Cut four 1¾" diameter branches for legs A, each 20" long.
2. Cut two 2" diameter branches for arms AA, each 24" long.
3. Cut four 1¼" diameter branches for side beams B, each 14¾" long.
4. Cut two 1½" diameter branches for front beams C, each 34½" long.
5. Cut one 1½" diameter branch for back bottom beam CC, 33" long.
6. Cut two 1¼" diameter branches for back supports D, each 38" long.
7. Cut one 1¼" diameter branch for seat support E, 36¾" long.
8. Cut two 1" diameter branches for braces F, each 22½" long.
9. Cut two or three ¾" diameter pliable branches for back G, each 8' long.
10. Cut 11 ¾" diameter pliable branches for seat/back GG, each 38" long.
11. Cut one ¾" diameter branch for seat rim H, 38" long.
12. Cut and split one ½" diameter branch for arm wraps HH, 35" long.
13. Cut one 1½" diameter branch for front beam brace I, 6" long.

Laying Out the Sub-Assembly
1. Using a pencil, mark a point on arm AA 5" from the back. Place the top of back leg A at this spot. From the top, drill pilot holes and nail arm AA to leg A using a #10p nail.
2. Using a pencil, mark a spot 3" from the front of arm AA. Place the top of front leg A under the arm at this spot. From the top, drill pilot holes and nail in place.
3. Repeat steps 1 and 2 above with the remaining arms and legs.
4. Butt beam B between front and back legs A, 5" down from the top of the legs. Drill pilot holes and nail in place from the outside of the legs. The top side beam is now in place.
5. Butt bottom side beam B between front and back legs A, 8" up from the bot-

tom of the legs. Drill pilot holes and nail in place from the outside of the legs. The bottom side beam is now in place.

6. Repeat steps 3 and 4, butting, drilling pilot holes, and nailing the remaining two side beams to the other leg/arm construction.

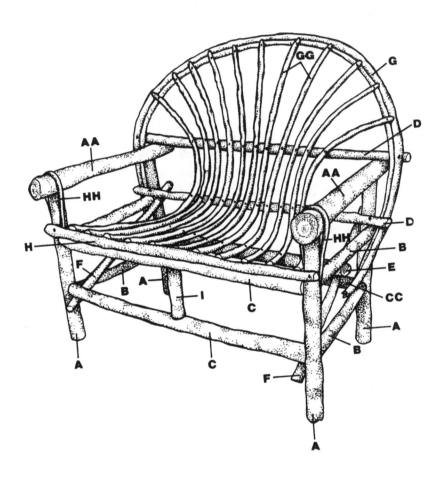

Joining the Sub-Assemblies

1. Butt top front beam C between the inside of the two front legs at the same points as top side beams B. Drill pilot holes and nail in place from the outside of the legs.
2. Repeat step 1 with bottom front beam C, placing it at the same point as bottom side beam B.
3. Butt back bottom beam CC between the inner back legs at approximately the

same point that the bottom side beams meet the back legs. Drill pilot holes and nail in place from the sides of both back legs.

4. Overlap lower back support branch D across both top side beams B.

5. Drill pilot holes through back support branch D into the back legs at a 45° angle. Using a #6p or #8p nail, join lower back support branch D to the back legs.

6. Overlap upper back support beam D across the top rear of both arms, 2" from the ends of the arms. Drill pilot holes and nail in place from the top of back support D into the arms.

7. Turn your construction over so that the underside is visible. Overlap seat support E approximately halfway along the bottom edge of top side beams B. Drill pilot holes and nail in place from the underside, being careful not to come through the top side beams.

8. Turn the settee on its side. Position brace F along the inner front leg, resting it just below the bottom of front beam C and allowing approximately 2" to extend. Along the side of the back leg and resting under lower seat support E, position the other end of brace F, allowing approximately 2" to extend.

9. Drill and nail brace F in place through the brace into the front and back legs from the inside.

10. Repeat with the other brace F.

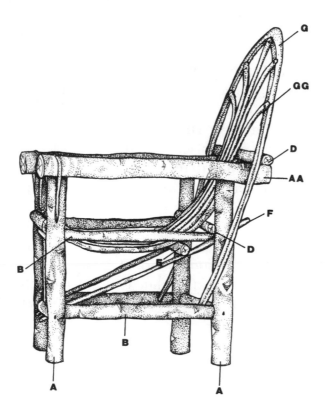

Adding the Top

1. Select one top branch G, drill pilot holes, and nail one end of G to the inside of lower side beam B, then to the outside of lower back support beam D and to the inside of upper back support beam D.
2. Gently bend top branch G to form an arch. The top of the arch should be approximately 36" high. Fasten the other end of G to the opposite side in the same manner.
3. Repeat steps 1 and 2 with the remaining one or two top branches G, placing the additional branches inside the existing arched top. Drill pilot holes and nail top G parts to one another using 1" finishing nails.

Adding the Seat/Back

1. Beginning in the center and working outward, position one seat branch GG along the top of front top beam C. Drill pilot holes and nail in place. Continue to gently bend GG toward the back, first drilling and nailing to E, then drilling and nailing to each of the two back supports D, and finally, drilling and nailing to G.
2. Repeat with remaining seat/back branches GG, forming a fan-shape as pictured.
3. Position seat rim H along the front exposed ends of seat branches GG. Drill pilot holes and nail in place through the front of H into each GG branch.
4. Position front beam brace I between top and bottom front beams C. Drill pilot holes and nail in place through the top of the upper beam and the bottom of the lower beam.
5. Wrap one end of arm wrap HH along the inside edge of the front leg. Drill pilot holes and nail in place. Carefully wrap HH over the top of the arm. Drill pilot holes and nail to the outside of the front leg.
6. Repeat step 5 with remaining arm wrap HH along the opposite leg.

Finishing

The settee may be finished in the same manner as the occasional chair. It is an excellent piece to paint in a combination of bright colors if you decide to use it in a den or family room. Painting the settee white is also a good choice, whether your taste runs to English traditional, country French, or a more eclectic style.

BENTWOOD CAMP CHAIR

This four-foot-tall chair was my first design and, with a seat cushion, serves as a surprisingly comfortable desk chair. Its magnificent proportions and lyrical shapes make it worth building as a dining chair, or as extra seating in the living room or bedroom.

MATERIALS

Use such woods as beech, cedar, birch, or willow. Lengths will range from 18" to 48", and diameters from ¾" to 2". You'll need 15 similar branches of willow (or any pliable wood) 30" long and ¾" in diameter for the seat supports (see Bentwood Camp Chair Cutting Chart). Galvanized flathead nails in assorted sizes (#4p, #6p, #8p, and #10p) are also necessary.

T O O L S

- ◆ Single bit axe for felling trees
- ◆ Crosscut hand saw
- ◆ Clippers or garden shears
- ◆ Ruler or measuring tape
- ◆ Marking pencil
- ◆ Drill with a selection of bits
- ◆ Hammer
- ◆ Safety goggles
- ◆ Work gloves
- ◆ Pocket knife (optional)
- ◆ Key-hole saw (optional)
- ◆ Drift punch (optional)

B E N T W O O D   C A M P   C H A I R   C U T T I N G   C H A R T

NAME OF PART	QUANTITY	DIAMETER (INCHES)	LENGTH (INCHES)	DESCRIPTION
Front leg/arm supports A	2	1	27	similar, forked, naturally bent
Back legs B	2	2	47	straight
Arms C	2	1½	20	smooth
Beams D	3	1½	23	hardwood
Back beams D1	1	2	17½	hardwood
Side rails E	2	1¼	20	hardwood
Stretchers F	4	¾	50	hardwood
Top rail G	1	1¾	21	hardwood
Seat supports H	15	¾	50	pliable
Armbraces I	2	1	23	forked
Bottom braces	2	¾	22–27	hardwood

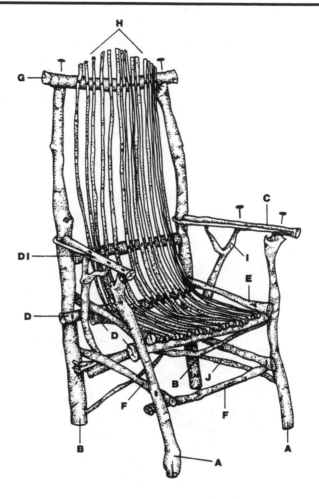

DIRECTIONS

Cutting the Branches

1. Carefully select two similar, naturally bent, forked branches that are 1" in diameter for the front leg/arm supports A. These pieces are an important part of your finished work. Cut them each 27" long.
2. Cut two relatively straight 2" diameter branches for back legs B, each 47" long.
3. Cut two smooth 1½" diameter branches for arms C, each 20" long.
4. Cut three 1½" diameter branches for beams D, each 23" long.
5. Cut one 2" diameter branch for back beam D1, 17½" long.

6. Cut two 1¼" diameter branches for side rails E, each 20" long.
7. Cut four ¾" diameter branches for stretchers F, each 22" long.
8. Cut one 1¾" diameter branch for the backrest's top rail G, 21" long.
9. Cut 15 branches ¾" in diameter for seat supports H, each 50" long.
10. Cut two forked branches 1" in diameter for arm braces I, each 23" long.
11. Cut two branches ¾" in diameter for bottom braces J, each 26" long.

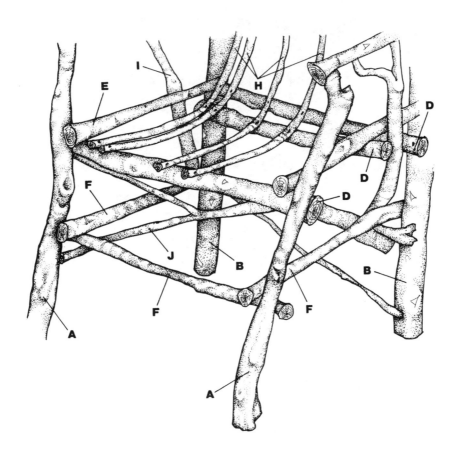

Laying Out the Sub-Assembly
1. Using a pencil, mark the inside of front leg A and the inside of back leg B 16" from the bottom.
2. Butt side rail E between A and B at the pencil marks. Drill pilot holes and nail in place.
3. Repeat step 2 with the remaining A, B, and E branches.

Joining the Sub-Assemblies
1. Overlap one beam D across the two front legs A, 17" from the bottom. Drill and nail in place from the inside.
2. Repeat step 1 at back legs B.
3. Overlap and lay side rail E across front and back beams D, butting against front and back legs A and B. Drill pilot holes through E and D, and nail in place. Drill pilot holes from the inside through E and front leg A, and through E and back leg B. Then nail in place from the inside.
4. Repeat step 3 with the other side.
5. Turn your construction over. Overlap the remaining beam D approximately 5" from lower back beam D across the two side rails E. Drill and nail in place. Stand the chair up.
6. Using a pencil, make a mark 10" from the bottom of the two front legs A. Overlap one stretcher F at the pencil mark. Drill pilot holes and nail in place from the inside.
7. Repeat step 6 at back legs B, adding stretcher F.
8. Overlap a side stretcher F across the front and back stretchers you have just applied. Drill pilot holes and nail in place from the underside.
9. Repeat step 8 at the opposite side.

Bracing
1. Turn the construction over. Overlap forked braces J on top of front and back stretchers F at a diagonal. Drill pilot holes and nail in place from the underside. Where to place the braces is up to you, since forked branches vary greatly.
2. At this point, test the construction for weight-bearing capacity. Add any additional braces that may be required.

Adding the Arms

1. Position arms C on top of front leg/arm supports A, and butt them against back legs B. Drill pilot holes and nail in place from the back of B, and through the top of A. (If the front legs are forked at the top, add another nail.)

2. Position forked arm brace I under arm C, with its bottom end overlapping the inside of back stretchers F. Drill pilot holes and nail in place from the top of arms C, from the inside of stretchers F, and where I meets side rails E.

3. Test for strength and add extra nails if required.

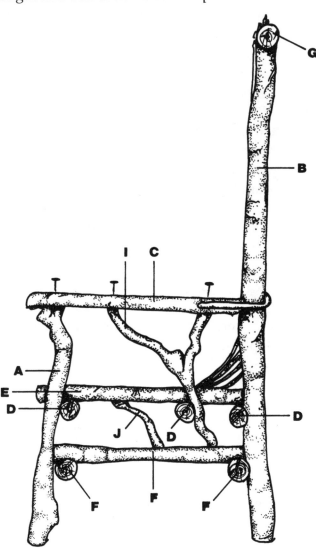

Adding the Seat

1. Overlap seatback top rail G across the extended ends of back legs B. Drill pilot holes and nail in place.

2. Butt back beam D1 between the two back legs B, 24" from the bottom. Drill pilot holes and nail in place from the outside of both back legs B.

3. Working from the front of the chair, beginning with the center twig and moving outward, attach pliable seat supports H to the front two beams D, using pilot hole and nail construction. Gently bend each H twig in a comfortable curve and attach to D1 and G using pilot hole and nail construction.

4. Cut the front ends of the H twigs so that they are even. Trim the top ends as shown, or in any fashion you desire.

Finishing

This distinctive chair, with its curves and bends, is best left in its natural state, so that the color and texture of the wood can be fully appreciated. It is remarkably cozy as is, but you may wish to include a seat cushion.

WATTLE ARM CHAIR

Named for its wonderful weaving, the wattle chair recalls the border fences that dot the English countryside. Wattling describes poles or stakes interwoven with twigs for making fences or walls. The art of wattling seems to be enjoying a revival as home gardeners learn more about transforming twigs and branches into all sorts of functional items. As wattle weaving increases in popularity, there is renewed interest in coppicing.

Coppicing is a simple timber-harvesting system based on the ability of deciduous hardwood trees to send up new growth from a cut stump. After a tree is cut, sprouts begin to shoot up from the old stump. Encourage coppicing by permitting sprouts to grow throughout the summer. When the leaves begin to turn color and drop, prune the slow-growing stems, and leave three or four of the most vigorous ones. These stronger trunks will be somewhat uniform and grow rapidly. Cut the stems when they reach the appropriate diameter and length for your purpose; usually within two or three years. Willow, alder, poplar, cottonwood and locust coppice best of all.

A small coppice lot would be ideal as a harvest for this chair as well as fencing and years of twig building.

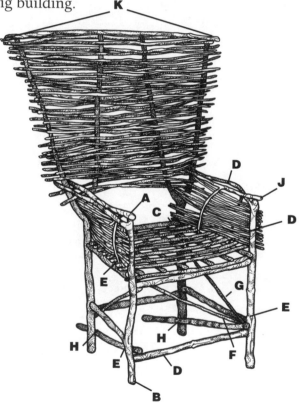

MATERIALS

For the body of the chair locate pliable twigs such as willow, alder or cottonwood, ranging from 16" to 30" in length and ½" to 1½" in diameter. You will also need two forked pliable twigs, at least 40" long and 1" to 1½" in diameter. You will also need two forked pliable twigs, at least 40" long and 1" to 1½" in diameter. For back and arm weaving, gather an assortment of ¼" to ½" diameter straight, pliable branches; 75 to 100 branches, 22" to 42" long constitute a good selection. The seat requires fourteen ¼" diameter straight twigs, 24" long. Keep on hand a selection of galvanized flat head nails, 1½" galvanized roofing nails, and 1½" finishing nails.

TOOLS

- Single bit axe for felling trees
- Cross cut hand saw
- Clippers or garden shears
- Ruler or measuring tape
- Marking pencil
- Drill with a selection of bits
- Hammer
- Safety goggles
- Work gloves
- Pocket knife (optional)

WATTLE ARM CHAIR CUTTING CHART

NAME OF PART	QUANTITY	DIAMETER (INCHES)	LENGTH (INCHES)	DESCRIPTION
Back legs A	2	1–1½	40	forked
Note: The following part B is more than one piece; the arm is a graceful branch growing out of the leg.				
Front leg/arms B	2	1–½	26 leg	similar, natural
Back beams C	3	1	20 arm	right angle
Front beams D	2	1	18	hardwood
Side stretchers E	4	1	21	hardwood
Front brace F	1	½	16	hardwood
Side braces G	2	½	26	pliable
Balance braces H	2	¾–1	23	pliable
Seat branches I	15	½	28	hardwood

NAME OF PART	QUANTITY	DIAMETER (INCHES)	LENGTH (INCHES)	DESCRIPTION
Arm rests J	2	½–¾	21	*straight/pliable
Top rail K	1	½–¾	42	pliable
Back weaving	60	½	42	pliable
Arm weaving	1	¼	22	pliable

DIRECTIONS

Cutting the Branches

1. Carefully select two similar, 1" to 1½" diameter, forked branches for the back legs A. Cut the back legs A to be 24" long from the end to the crotch in the fork, with the forked ends extending another 30", thus having the pieces measure a total of 54". These parts determine the scale and shape of the finished chair. Take your time to locate the right pieces.
2. Cut two straight 1" to 1½" diameter branches with natural forked right angles (see diagram #1) for the front leg/arms B, each 26" long with an extending 20" arm.
3. Cut three hardwood 1" diameter branches for the back beams C, each 18" long.
4. Cut two hardwood 1" diameter branches for the front beams D, each 21" long.
5. Cut four hardwood 1" diameter branches for the side stretchers E, each 16" long.
6. Cut one pliable ½" diameter branch for the front brace F, 26" long.
7. Cut two pliable ½" diameter branches for the side braces G, each 23" long.
8. Cut two strong hardwood ¾" to 1" diameter branches for the balance braces H, each 28" long.
9. Cut fourteen straight ½" diameter branches for the seat I, each 24" long.
10. Cut two straight, pliable branches with extending limbs (see diagram #2), ½" to ¾" diameter, for the arm rests J, each 21" long.
11. Cut one pliable ½" to ¾" diameter branch for the top rail K, 42" long.
12. Cut at least sixty ½" diameter very pliable branches for the back weaving, each 42" long.
13. Cut at least forty ¼" diameter very pliable branches for the arm weaving, each 22" long.

ARMREST J

FRONT LEG / ARM B

Laying Out the Sub-Assembly

1. Using a pencil, mark the inside of both back legs A 7" from the bottom.
2. Butt one back beam C between both back legs A at the pencil marks. Drill pilot holes and nail in place from the outside using 1 ½" roofing nails.
3. Mark the inside of both back legs A 10" from the installed beam C. Cut the second back beam C between back legs A at these marks, and repeat step 2.
4. Mark the inside of both front legs/arm B 5" from the bottom. Butt one front beam D between front legs B at the pencil marks. Repeat step 2.
5. Mark the inside of both front leg/arms B 10" from the installed lower front beam D. Butt the second front beam D between B at these points and repeat step 2.

Joining the Sub-Assemblies

1. Butt one side stretcher E between the front leg B, 7" from the bottom and back leg A, 8" from the bottom. Drill pilot holes and nail in place from the front of legs B and the back of legs A.
2. Repeat step 1 with another side stretcher E.
3. Butt the third side stretcher E between the front leg B, and the back leg A at approximately 10" up from the lower E stretcher already installed. Drill and nail in place as in step 1.
4. Repeat with the remaining side stretcher E.
5. Overlap the extended arm B against the back leg A. Drill and nail in place from the outside.

Bracing

1. Turn the construction on its side. Diagonally overlap side braces G, at the top inside of back leg A (just under back beam C) and front leg B.
2. Repeat step 1 on the opposite side.
3. Place the construction face down. Overlap front brace F on top of front leg B and upper front beam D at an angle. Drill pilot holes and nail in place from the inside. Note: You may decide to add a second crossing brace at this time.
4. Return the construction to its side. Diagonally overlap balance braces H from top of front beam D to the inside of back leg A. Using pilot hole and nail construction, nail in place from the inside approximately 3" from the bottom of the back leg.

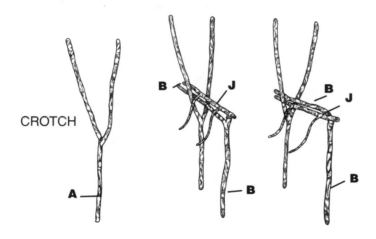

Adding the Seat

1. Stand the construction upright. Evenly space six seat branches I, and overlap them on both top back beam C and top front beam D. They should extend 1".
2. Using pilot hole and nail construction, nail the seat branches I to the back beam C.
3. Place one seat branch I under the front ends of the installed seat parts, close to the top front beam D. Nail the seat branches to this branch from the underside at the points where they meet.
4. Overlap the remaining seat branches perpendicularly across the installed seat parts, equally spaced in grid. The branches should extend and rest on the top side stretchers E. Using the pilot hole and nail construction, attach the seat parts to each other at the points where they cross.

5. Butt the remaining back beam C between the back legs A, resting on top of the extended seat parts I. Drill and nail in place from the outside.

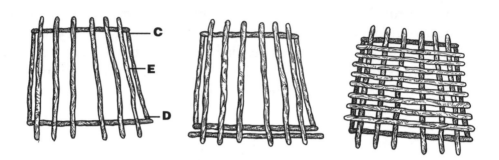

Weaving the Back

If your weaving branches are sufficiently supple and pliable and your forked back legs are nicely spaced, this should be quite easy as weaving is simpler than it looks. Begin from the bottom, and weave branch under and over the forks. Continue with a second branch above the first row of weaving, this time weaving over and under, and so on until you reach the top and are satisfied with the appearance. Overlap top rail K across the extended ends of the forked back legs A. Drill pilot holes and nail in place.

At this point, test the construction for weight-bearing capacity. Additional balance braces may be required.

Adding the arm weaving

1. Overlap arm rest J on top of front leg B and along the inside of back leg A approximately 30" from the bottom. It will probable rest on the sixth back weaving branch. Insert the extended branches of arm rest J between the top side stretcher E and the seat branch I.

Note: It is not necessary to nail the extended branches in place; if they are a snug fit the weaving should keep them in place. Drill and nail the overlapping arm rest in place on top of the front leg B and along the inside of the back leg A.

2. Using the 1/4" diameter arm weaving whips, begin weaving the sides from the bottom, outside of the front leg B, under and over the extended arm rest pieces, to rest inside the back leg A. As your weaving progresses, some of the

pieces will rest in the crotch of the forked back leg A. Continue weaving the sides until the entire area is filled in.

3. Trim the ends as shown.

Finishing

Nothing, except perhaps one plump cushion is required to enhance the natural beauty of this special piece. Boiled linseed oil mixed with a bit of turpentine or white vinegar may be wiped on to protect the bark, but it may dramatically change its color.

CHAISE LOUNGE

The arched back on this beautifully proportioned piece makes it a comfortable chaise lounge. Without the back and fitted with a mattress, it can become a daybed that is ideal for a den or cabin room. It is well worth the effort it takes to build this heirloom-quality piece, which will give years of service.

MATERIALS

Use such pliable branches as willow, alder, or cedar. Lengths should range from 72" to 10" and diameters from ½" to 1". You'll also need two 72" forked pliable branches. A selection of very flexible branches, as long as possible and ¼" to ½" in diameter, will be needed to wrap the arched back. You will also need hardwood (such as beech, birch, or cherry) in lengths ranging from 16" to 70" and ½" to ¾" in diameter. Galvanized flathead nails in assorted sizes (#2p, #4p, #5p, #6p, and #10p) are also required.

TOOLS

- Single bit axe for felling trees
- Crosscut hand saw
- Clippers or garden shears
- Ruler or measuring tape
- Marking pencil
- ⅜" variable-speed drill
- Hammer
- Safety goggles
- Work gloves

CHAISE LOUNGE CUTTING CHART

NAME OF PART	QUANTITY	DIAMETER (INCHES)	LENGTH (INCHES)	DESCRIPTION
Legs A	6	1¾	16	hardwood
Back support beam B1	1	1½	27	hardwood
Cross beams B	6	1¾	24	hardwood
Arched back C	4	½–1	120 (10')	pliable
Seat supports D	5	¾–1	72	pliable
Seat supports D	2	¾–1	72	forked, pliable
Top side rails E	2	1¾	60	hardwood
Lower side rails EE	4	1½	45	hardwood
Long brace X	1	½	55	hardwood
Short brace XX	1	¾	25	hardwood
Wrap branches	4–5	¼–½	as long as possible	very flexible

DIRECTIONS

Cutting the Branches

1. Cut six 1¾" diameter branches for legs A, each 16" long.
2. Cut one 1½" diameter branch for back support beam B1, 27" long.

3. Cut six 1¾" diameter branches for cross beams B, each 24" long.
4. Cut four ½" to 1" diameter pliable branches for arched back C, each at least 10' long.
5. Cut seven ¾" to 1" diameter pliable branches for seat supports D, each 72" long. Two of these should be forked branches.
6. Cut two 1¾" diameter branches for top side rails E, each 60" long.
7. Cut four 1½" diameter branches for lower side rails EE, each 45" long.
8. Cut one ½" diameter branch for long brace X, 55" long.
9. Cut one ¾" diameter branch for short brace XX, 25" long.

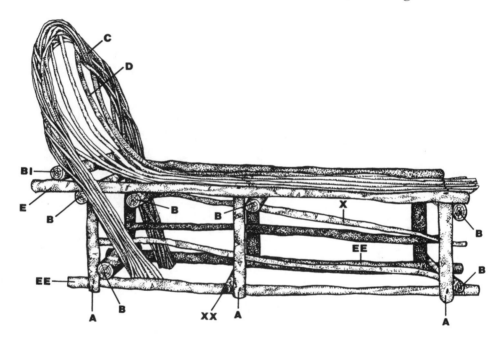

Laying Out the Sub-Assembly

1. Lay one top side rail E on your worktable. Butt one front leg A under top side rail E 5" from the end. Join with pilot hole and nail construction through the top of top side rail E.
2. Butt and join one center leg A in the same manner 20" back from the front leg.
3. Butt and join one back leg A in the same manner 20" back from the center leg.
4. With the first A and E construction lying on the worktable, overlap one lower side rail EE across the three installed legs, 8" below the top side rail. Using pi-

lot hole and nail construction, join side rail EE to each leg A at their meeting point.

5. Overlap lower side rail EE across the three installed legs, 2" from the bottom of the legs. Using pilot hole and nail construction, join lower side rail EE to each leg A at their meeting point.

6. Repeat steps 1 through 5 for the opposite side, with the remaining legs A, top side rail E, and lower side rails EE.

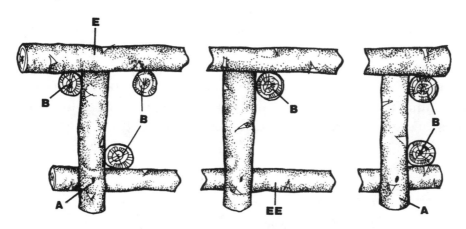

Joining the Sub-Assemblies

1. With the two sub-assemblies placed 20" apart and upside down, overlap one cross beam B across the two front legs and across the underside of top side rails E. Join cross beam B to legs A and top side rails E using pilot hole and nail construction. Nail B to A from the front and B to E from the underside.

2. Add the second cross beam B just in front of the center leg in the same manner.

3. Join the third beam to rails E 15" behind the second cross beam B, also from the underside.

4. Butt the fourth cross beam B behind the back legs and under the top rail E. Again, join in the same manner as the front beam.

5. Turn the construction right side up. Overlap the fifth cross beam B cross the two lower side rails EE and in front of the two front legs. Using pilot hole and nail construction, join B to A from the front and B to EE from the top.

6. Overlap the sixth cross beam B across the two lower side rails EE and in front of the two back legs. Using pilot hole and nail construction, join B to A from the front and B to EE from the top.

7. Place back support beam B1 across the back ends of the two top side rail E, 11" from the back ends of E. Using pilot hole and nail construction, join B1 to the two E branches from the top of B1.

Adding the Branches
1. Turn the construction upside down. With the front facing you, position long brace X inside the front left leg, diagonally under the cross beams B to the back right leg. Using pilot hole and nail construction, join long brace X to the front left leg and the back right leg. Test for stability and add nails to the cross beams B if required.
2. With the front of the construction still facing you, place short brace XX behind center cross beam B on the right side. Position it across and down, behind the center leg on the opposite side. Using pilot hole and nail construction, join XX to B and A. Test for stability, adding extra nails if required.

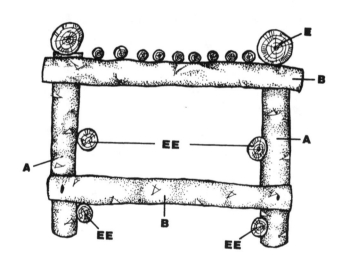

Adding the Back Bows
1. Position one pliable back branch C inside bottom lower side rail EE. Bring it outside top side rail EE, against rear cross beam B, and carefully ease it back to rest in front of back support beam B1. Drill and nail in place to B1. Carefully bend back branch C upward, forming an arch. Join to the opposite side in the same manner.

2. Add the remaining back bows C in the same manner, as close to one another as possible, but do not nail in place until later.

Attaching the Seat
1. Working from the center, position first seat support branch D on top of cross beams B. Using pilot hole and nail construction, join D to the upper three cross beams B. Slant the seat support branch back and insert it between the back bows.
2. Position two forked seat supports D on either side of the center seat support, with the forks at the head. Drill and nail in place as above.
3. Repeat step 1 with the remaining four seat supports.
4. Using pilot hole and nail construction, join seat supports D to back arched bow C.
5. Join arched bows C to each other at various locations to ensure stability.

Wrapping the Top
1. Wrap one end of a ¼" to ½" diameter pliable wrap branch around the four arched branch tops near back support beam B1. Weave it under and over back bows C, between seat supports D, and tuck in at the opposite side near B1. Continue to wrap and weave two or three other pliable branches around back bows C to stabilize them.

Finishing
The timeless appeal and lasting beauty of the chaise lounge will probably convince you to leave it in its natural state. Selecting the right cushion and pillows will add comfort, whether your chaise lounge is on a porch or in the living room. Consider using fabric from the wide array of patterned sheets that are available. With its generous width, inexpensive sheeting adds decorating impact and can be changed often.

FOLDING CHAIR

This chair has numerous precise parts that allow it to fold properly. If you are familiar with an electric saw, it can make the job go faster. Do not let the number of branches required to make this chair keep you from trying it. Once the branches are cut and drilled, they are simply strung on threaded rods. The placement and piecing technique is adapted from a South American Indian design, truly an engineering marvel.

MATERIALS

You can use beech, birch, cherry, or any hardwood. You will need lengths from 7" to 53" in diameters of 1¼" to 1½". You will also require four threaded, ¼" diameter metal rods, one 12" long, one 14" long, and two 25" long. Eight nuts and washers to fit the threaded rods, one 12" wooden dowel that is ½" in diameter, and wood glue will also be essential.

TOOLS

- Single bit axe for felling trees
- Crosscut hand saw
- Electric circular saw (optional)
- Drill and ⁵⁄₁₆" to ⅜" woodboring bit
- Ruler or measuring tape
- Marking pencil
- Safety goggles
- Work gloves

FOLDING CHAIR CUTTING CHART

NAME OF PART	QUANTITY	DIAMETER (INCHES)	LENGTH (INCHES)	DESCRIPTION
Front legs A	2	1¼	53	hardwood
Back legs B	2	1½	30	hardwood
Back leg rest C	2	1¼	28	hardwood
Back D	6	1¼–1½	30	hardwood
Seat braces E	11	¾–1½	7	hardwood
Seat F	8	1¼	14	hardwood

DIRECTIONS

Cutting the Branches

1. Cut two 1¼" diameter branches for front legs A, each 53" long.
2. Cut two 1½" diameter branches for back legs B, each 30" long.
3. Cut two 1¼" diameter branches for back leg rest C, each 28" long.
4. Cut six 1¼" to 1½" diameter branches for back D, each 30" long.
5. Cut 11 approximately equal ¾" to 1½" diameter branches for seat braces E, each 7" long.
6. Cut eight 1¼" diameter branches for seat F, each 14" long.

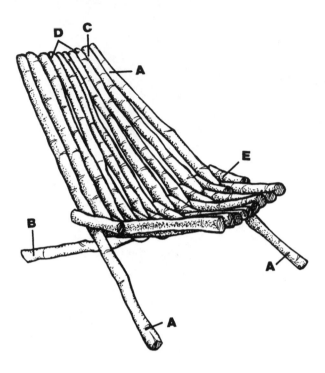

Drilling the Holes

1. Assemble the 11 seat brace parts E. Using a pencil, mark each part 1" in from both ends. Using the drill and woodboring bit, drill holes through the center of each branch at the 1" mark on both sides. Continue to drill the holes on all 11 branches.

2. Assemble the six back parts D. Mark each end at 1" as above. Drill all 12 holes.

3. Assemble the two back leg rest parts C. Mark each end at 1" as in step 1 above. Drill all four holes.

4. Assemble the two front leg parts A. Mark at 1" from one end, and at 18" from the opposite end. Drill all four holes.

5. Assemble the two back leg parts B. Mark at 1" from one end, and at 18" from the opposite end. Drill all four holes.

6. Assemble the eight seat parts F. Mark at 1" from one end, and at 3" from the opposite end. Drill all 16 holes.

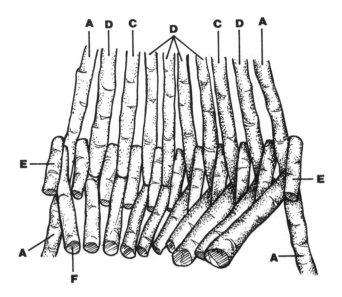

Arranging the Parts

1. Before "threading" the parts, you should arrange them in their proper order on the floor or worktable to achieve the most pleasing placement. Place one branch E down for the chair back. Line up the holes of one branch A with the holes of E, laying them beside one another. Place the remaining parts in the following order: E,D,E,C,E,D,E,D,E,D,E,D,E,C,E,D,E,A,E. For the seat: E,F,E,F,E,B,E,F,E,F,E,F,E,F,E,B,E,F,E,F,E. It is generally a good idea to place the heavier pieces toward the outside. When you are satisfied with the placement of the parts, you are ready to begin putting your chair together.

2. Next you will need to countersink drill the outermost holes on the assembly so that the threaded rod nuts and rod ends will be hidden from view. Countersunk holes should be ½" deep and ½" in diameter. Using the countersink bit, drill in both holes of the two seat brace parts E, in the two top holes in both front leg parts A, and in the two top holes in the two seat parts F.

Threading the Parts

1. Place a nut and washer on one end of each of the four threaded rods.

2. To assemble the back, start with one 25" rod, and string the parts in the following order: countersunk E, then A,E,D,E,C,E,D,E,D,E,D,E,D,E,C,E,D,E, A and countersunk E.

3. Force the parts together for a snug fit. Thread a nut and washer on the exposed rod. Thread the 12" rod through the top holes of parts A and parts D. Secure the ends of the rod with the nut and washer.

4. Place a nut and washer on one end of the remaining 25" rod. Arrange one seat part F inside the partially-threaded E part at its 3" predrilled hole, matching up the holes. Thread the rod through the seat parts in the following order: countersunk E, then F,E,F,E,B,E,F,E,F,E,F,E,F,E,B,E,F,E,F and countersunk E.

5. Force the parts together for a snug fit. Thread a nut and washer on the exposed rod. Thread the 14" rod through the bottom holes of part F and parts B. Secure the ends of the rods with the nut and washer.

6. Cut the wooden dowel to fit the depth of the eight countersunk holes. Plug the holes to cover the nuts and the rod ends. Using the wood glue, fasten the dowel plugs in place.

Finishing

This folding chair is useful for winter storage and extra seating. If you are using it out-of-doors for a prolonged period, spray it with a mixture of linseed oil and turpentine or several coats of polyurethane. Fitted with plump pillows, the folding chair adds character to an otherwise plain room.

OCCASIONAL CHAIR

This 18"-wide chair is based on a formula that was popular at summer camps and in bungalows during the 1920s and 1930s. Its graceful curves continue to be inviting. The chair's simple proportions help to create harmony both indoors and out.

MATERIALS

You will require 7 pliable branches, such as cedar or willow, ranging from 38" to 78" long with diameters of ¾" and any hardwood branches ranging from 6" to 24" long with diameters of 1" to 2". Galvanized flathead nails in assorted sizes (#4p, #6p, #8p, and #10p) and about 24 1" finishing nails will also be necessary.

TOOLS

- ◆ Single bit axe for felling trees
- ◆ Crosscut hand saw
- ◆ Clippers or garden shears
- ◆ Ruling or measuring tape
- ◆ Marking pencil
- ◆ ⅜" variable-speed drill
- ◆ Hammer
- ◆ Safety goggles
- ◆ Work gloves
- ◆ Crosscut skill saw (optional)
- ◆ Key-hole saw (optional)
- ◆ Pocket knife (optional)

OCCASIONAL CHAIR CUTTING CHART

NAME OF PART	QUANTITY	DIAMETER (INCHES)	LENGTH (INCHES)	DESCRIPTION
Legs A	4	1¾	20	hardwood
Arms AA	2	2	24	hardwood
Side beams B	4	1¼	14¾	hardwood
Front beams C	2	1½	19¾	hardwood
Back bottom beam CC	1	1½	18	hardwood
Back supports D	2	1¼	24	hardwood
Seat support E	1	1¼	21	hardwood
Braces F	2	1	24	hardwood
Back G	2–3	¾	75	pliable
Seat/back GG	5	¾	38	pliable
Seat rim H	1	½	24	pliable
Arm wrap HH	1	½	35	pliable
Front beam brace I	1	1½	6	hardwood

DIRECTIONS

Cutting the Branches
1. Cut four 1¾" diameter branches for legs A, each 20" long.
2. Cut two 2" diameter branches for arms AA, each 24" long.
3. Cut four 1¼" diameter branches for side beams B, each 14¾" long.
4. Cut two 1½" diameter branches for front beams C, each 19¾" long.
5. Cut one 1½" diameter branch for back bottom beam CC, 18" long.
6. Cut two 1¼" diameter branches for back supports D, each 24" long.
7. Cut one 1¼" diameter branch for seat support E, 21" long.
8. Cut two 1" diameter branches for braces F, each 24" long.
9. Cut two or three ¾" diameter pliable branches for back G, each 75" long.

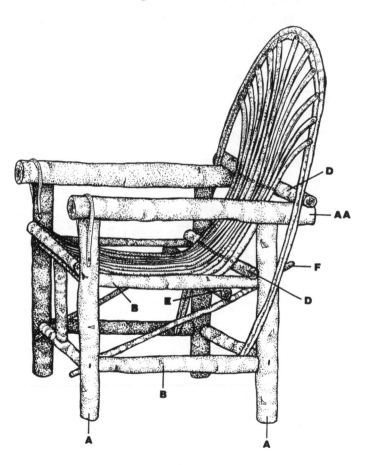

10. Cut five ¾" diameter pliable branches for seat/back GG, each 38" long.
11. Cut one ½" diameter branch for seat rim II, 24" long.
12. Cut and split one ½" diameter branch for arm wraps HH, 35" long.
13. Cut one 1½" diameter branch for front beam brace I, 6" long.

Laying Out the Sub-Assembly
1. Using a pencil, mark a spot along arm AA 5" from the end. Place the top of back leg A at this spot. From the top, drill and nail arm AA to leg A, using a #10p nail.
2. Using a pencil, mark a spot 3" from the front of arm AA. Place the top of front leg A under the arm at this spot. From the top, drill a pilot hole and nail in place.
3. Repeat steps 1 and 2 above with the remaining arms and legs.
4. Butt beam B between front and back legs A, 5" down from the top of the legs. Drill pilot holes and nail in place from the outside of the legs. The top side beam is now in place.
5. Butt bottom side beam B between front and back legs A, 8" up from the bottom of the legs. Drill pilot holes and nail in place from the outside of the legs. The bottom side beam is now in place.
6. Repeats steps 4 and 5, butting, drilling pilot holes, and nailing the remaining two side beams to the remaining leg/arm construction.

Joining the Sub-Assemblies
1. Butt top front beam C between the inside of the two front legs at approximately the same location as top side beams B. Drill pilot holes and nail in place from the outside of the legs.
2. Repeat step 1 with bottom front beam C.
3. Butt back bottom beam CC between the inner back legs at approximately the same location that the bottom side beams meet the back legs. Drill and nail in place from the sides of both back legs.
4. Overlap one back support branch D across both top side beams B.
5. Drill pilot holes through back support branch D into the back legs at a 45° angle. Using a #6p or #8p nail, fasten the back support branch to the back legs.
6. Overlap the remaining back support beam D across the rear top of both arms. Approximately 2" from the ends of the arms, drill pilot holes and nail in place (from the front of back support D into the arms).

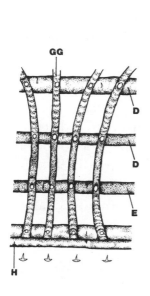

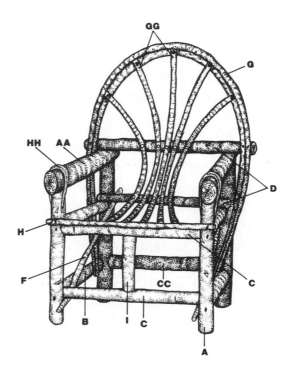

7. Turn your construction over so that the underside is visible. Overlap seat support E approximately halfway along the edge of top side beams B. Drill pilot holes and nail in place from the underside, being careful not to come through the top side beams.

8. Turn the chair on its side. Position brace F along the inner front leg, resting it just below the bottom of front beam C, allowing approximately 2" to extend downward. Rest the other end along the inner back leg just under lower seat support E, allowing approximately 2" to extend upward.

9. Drill pilot holes and nail brace F in place through the brace into the front and back legs from the inside.

10. Repeat steps 8 and 9 with remaining brace F.

Adding the Top

1. Select one top branch G. Drill pilot holes and nail G to the inside of lower side beam B, to the outside of lower back support beam D, and to the inside of upper back support beam D.

2. Gently bend top branch G to form an arch. The top of the arch should be approximately 36" high. Fasten the remaining end of G to the other leg and support beams as in step 1.

3. Repeat steps 1 and 2 with the remaining one or two top branches G, placing each additional arched branch inside the first arch. Drill pilot holes and nail top G parts to one another using 1" finishing nails.

Adding the Seat/Back

1. Beginning in the center and working outward, position each seat branch GG along the top of the front top beam C. Drill pilot holes and nail in place. Continue to gently bend GG toward the back, drilling pilot holes and nailing first to E, then drilling and nailing to each of the two back supports D. Finally, drill and nail to G.

2. Repeat with remaining seat/back branches GG, forming a fan-shape as shown.

3. Position seat rim H along the front extended ends of seat branches GG. Drill and nail in place through the front of H into each GG branch.

4. Position the front beam brace I between the top and bottom front beams C. Drill pilot holes and nail in place through the top of the upper beam and through the bottom of the lower beam.

5. Wrap one end of arm wrap HH along the inside edge of the front leg. Drill pilot holes and nail in place. Carefully wrap HH over the top of the arm. Drill pilot holes and nail in place to the outside of the front leg.

6. Repeat with remaining arm wrap HH on the opposite side.

Finishing

If you build the occasional chair out of cedar, it will be a beautiful pale blond color that is quite lovely left in its natural state. To preserve this color and to protect the wood for outdoor use, seal with several coats of polyurethane. To "age" the wood naturally, place the piece outdoors until it takes on a soft, silvery-grey sheen. This can then be sealed with a mixture of equal parts linseed oil and turpentine. With comfortable cushions added, these also make nice dining chairs or desk chairs.

UPHOLSTERED
VANITY CHAIR

Capture the romantic country spirit with this imaginative chair—even in the city! A bunch of pliable twigs, and scraps of vintage fabric are transformed into a whimsical seat, equally perfect for an elegant boudoir or a young girl's tea party.

MATERIALS

Collect two pliable, forked and branched twigs such as willow, alder or hazel, at least 72" long with diameters of 1" to 1¾" and hardwood branches 14" long with diameters of 1" to 1¾". You may also need an assortment of long straight green branches of willow, hazel or mulberry for some of the decorative arched back trim. A 3" thick log slice (or cut pine board) 12" in diameter, and a piece of ½" plywood, 12" in diameter are made into the seat. Use approximately ¾" of a yard of fabric and stuffing (or padding) for the upholstery. Galvanized flathead nails in assorted sizes (#4p, #6p, #8p, and #10p), upholstery or carpet tacks (¾" to 1") and 1" finishing nails will also be necessary.

TOOLS

- Single bit axe for felling trees
- Crosscut hand saw
- Clippers or garden shears
- Ruler or measuring tape
- Marking pencil
- ⅜" variable-speed drill
- Hammer
- Scissors
- Heavy-duty glue
- Staple gun and staples (optional)
- Pocket knife (optional)
- Safty goggles
- Work gloves
- Carpenter's glue (optional)

UPHOLSTERED VANITY CHAIR CUTTING CHART

NAME OF PART	QUANTITY	DIAMETER (INCHES)	LENGTH (INCHES)	DESCRIPTION
Front legs A	2	1–1¾	14	hardwood
Back legs/arched back B	2	1–1¾	72 (or more)	hardwood
Stretcher #1 C	1	1	11	hardwood
Stretcher #2 D	1	1	13	hardwood
Arched trim E	1–5	¼–¾	72	pliable

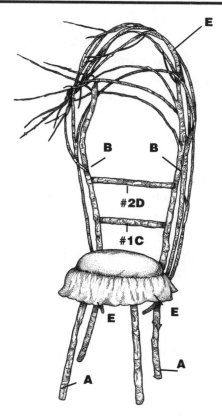

DIRECTIONS

Cutting the Branches

1. Cut two 1" to 1¾" diameter branches for front legs A, each 14" long.
2. Cut two 1" to 1¾" diameter pliable branches for the back legs/arched back B, each at least 72" long.
3. Cut one hardwood branch 1" in diameter for stretcher #1 C, 11" long.
4. Cut one hardwood branch 1" in diameter for stretcher #2 D, 13" long.
   Cut one or more pliable branches ¼"–¾" in diameter for optional arched trim E, at least 72" long.

Attaching the Front Legs to the Seat

1. Note: The front legs are attached on the *bottom* of the log slice. Place the 3" thick log slice (or cut pine board) face down on the work table. Using a pencil, mark two spots 2" from the front and from the side edge.

2. Select a bit slightly smaller than the diameter of the front legs to allow for a snug fit. Drill ¾" deep holes for the legs at the pencil marks.
3. Insert front legs A, by gently twisting them into the drilled openings. Use a squirt of glue in the hole and a dab on the leg if desired. Dip the leg in sawdust if it is too loose. Measure the legs to make sure they are of equal length.

Adding the Back Legs/Arched Back

Turn construction over so that the back is facing you.

1. Note: The back legs are attached to the *back* of the log slice, arranged 10" apart. Beginning at the center and working outward, position each back leg B along the side of the log slice.
2. Drill two pilot holes for each leg B through the log slice and nail in place. Allow the crowns of branches to remain as they are until you complete the next step.

Adding the Stretchers

1. Butt stretcher #1 C between the two extended back legs, 6" from the top of the seat. Using pilot hole and nail construction, nail in place from the outside of the legs.
2. Butt stretcher #2 D between the two extended back legs, 6" from stretcher #1 and fasten as in step 1.

Bending the Back

1. Carefully bend each extended crown branch toward the opposite back leg, arching the top as you go. Tuck the ends in front of the back legs and under the seat. Drill pilot holes and nail in place with finishing nails.
2. Add some arched pliable branches and nail in place with finishing nails, if needed.

Upholstering the Seat

1. Make a ½" hem on a strip of fabric 4" wide and 1½" to 2 yards long, and gather it evenly to create a ruffle. With upholstery or carpet tacks (or heavy-duty staples and a staple gun) attach the raw edge of the ruffle evening around the outer top edge of the log slice.
2. Place a piece of 13" to 15" square fabric on a work table with the right side down. Arrange one to two inches of pillow padding or stuffing on

top of the fabric. Place a thick piece of ½" plywood 12" in diameter on top of the padding. Pull the fabric edges up and attach the raw edges tightly around the circumference of the plywood, using the tacks or a staple gun and staples.

3. Stand ruffle-trimmed chair upright. Apply heavy-duty glue to the log slice and to the bottom of the plywood; press the two together. Place heavy books or any significant weight on top of the cushion and allow it to dry overnight.

CHILD'S CHAIR

This stout little chair is 15" wide, and is a good lesson in willow bending. Its design comprises three beautifully bowed pieces, forming the legs, arms, and back.

MATERIALS

Use any pliable branches such as willow or cedar, ranging in lengths from 48" to 64" and 1" diameter, for the back and arm/leg bows. Willow, or any hardwood branches ranging from 12" to 18" in length and ¾" to 1" in diameter can be used for the seat and stretchers. You will also need galvanized flathead nails in assorted sizes (#2p, #4p, and #6p), ½" to ¾" finishing nails, and 48" of heavy household string to aid in forming the bows.

TOOLS

- ♦ Single bit axe for felling trees
- ♦ Crosscut hand saw
- ♦ Clippers or garden shears
- ♦ Ruler or measuring tape
- ♦ Marking pencil
- ♦ Drill with a selection of bits
- ♦ Hammer
- ♦ Safety goggles
- ♦ Work gloves
- ♦ Pocket knife (optional)

CHILD'S CHAIR CUTTING CHART

NAME OF PART	QUANTITY	DIAMETER (INCHES)	LENGTH (INCHES)	DESCRIPTION
Back A	1	1	55	pliable
Arm/leg bows B	2	1	41	pliable
Front stretchers C	2	1	16	hardwood
Back stretchers CC	2	1	14	hardwood
Side stretchers D	2	1	13	hardwood
Top side stretchers DD	2	1	12	hardwood
Seat E	11–13	¾	14	hardwood
Seat-edge trim F	1	1	15	split in half lengthwise
Back trim O	1	½	44	pliable

DIRECTIONS

Cutting the Branches

The back and arm/leg bows are cut longer than their finished size to allow for bending and stabilizing.

    1. Cut one 1" diameter pliable branch for back A, 63" long.

2. Cut two 1" diameter pliable branches for arm/leg bows B, 48" long.
3. Cut two 1" diameter branches for front stretchers C, each 16" long.
4. Cut two 1" diameter branches for back stretchers CC, each 14" long.
5. Cut two 1" diameter branches for side stretchers D, each 13" long.
6. Cut two 1" diameter branches for top side stretchers DD, each 12" long.
7. Cut 11 to 13 ¾" diameter branches for seat E, each 14" long.
8. Cut and split in half one 1" diameter branch for the seat-edge trim F, 15" long.
9. Cut one pliable ½" diameter branch for back trim O, 44" long.

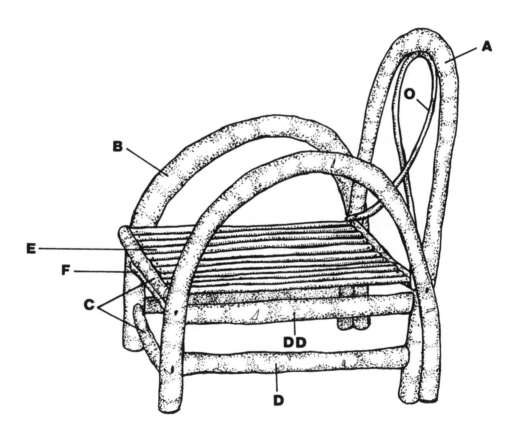

Laying Out the Sub-Assembly: Forming the Back
1. Carefully bend the back bow A to form an arched shape. Tie a string tightly between the ends, leaving a 15" opening between the two ends of A.
2. Repeat the above procedure with the two arm/leg bows B, leaving a 14" opening between the ends.

3. Drill pilot holes 19" down from the top center of back bow A on each side.

4. Drill pilot holes through the ends of top back stretcher CC. Butt against back hoop A and nail in place.

5. Repeat with bottom back stretcher CC, placing it 7½" below top bark stretcher CC.

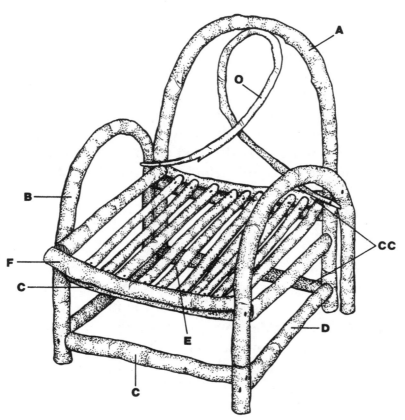

Adding Arms/Legs

1. Drill and nail arm/leg bow B in place along the outside of the back bow A, just above the nails holding the back stretchers in place.

2. Adjust the second arm/leg bow B so that it is equal with the already attached bow. Repeat step 1 above.

3. Butt top front stretcher C between the front of the two arm/leg bows. Drill pilot holes and nail in place from the outside of the arm/leg bow B.

4. Repeat with the remaining bottom front stretcher C, placing it 7½" from the top front stretcher.

5. Butt top side stretcher DD along the inside of front arm/leg bow B and the inside of back A. Drill pilot holes and nail in place from the outside.
6. Repeat with bottom side stretcher D.
7. Add top side stretcher DD and bottom side stretcher D to the opposite side in the same manner.

Adding the Bark
1. Working from the center twig outward, arrange all seat elements E, over lapping the tops of front and back stretchers C and CC.
2. When you are satisfied with the placement, drill pilot holes and nail in place from the top, securing the seat elements to the top stretchers.
3. Adjust split seat-edge trim F to fit the front of the protruding ends of the seat twigs. Using four or five nails, drill and nail in place from the front.
4. Repeat with the remaining split trim F along the back seat.

Adding the Back Trim
1. Carefully bend and loop back trim O, as pictured.
2. Using 1" finishing nails, drill pilot holes and nail in place along the front of back A and under the center of the bend in the bow.
3. Leave the strings in place until the wood is seasoned. When you are satisfied that the bows will retain their shape, usually in four to six weeks, remove the string and cut the ends of legs A and B so that the chair stands approximately 23" high from the center of the bow to the bottom of the legs (so that the arm/leg bows are 17" high).

Finishing
The back opening of the chair acts as a framework that permits you to construct and arrange original components. You might consider adding slats or forked branches. Painted a bright color, with a comfortable cushion, the chair will be a welcome and lasting gift. The chair can also be used as a plant or magazine stand. Don't forget to make one for a doll collector friend.

Child's Ladder-Back Chair

This slim, graceful chair measures 27" high, with a seat that is 12" deep and 10" wide. It makes a welcome addition to any room of the house. The chair's sturdy seat is constructed of ¼" slats. Perhaps you will want to make two or three so you can invite several small friends to an old-fashioned tea party. Hanging from a peg on the front door, a ladder-back chair signals a cheerful welcome. This is a wonderful project for grandparents!

MATERIALS

You will need pliable or hardwood twigs, such as alder or willow, ranging from 8" to 27" in length and ½" to ¾" in diameter. You will also need two forked pliable twigs, 27" long, five ¼" box-wood or pine boards, 12" long and 2" wide, and galvanized flathead nails (#2p and #4p).

TOOLS

- Crosscut hand saw
- Garden shears or clippers
- Drill with a selection of bits
- Pencil
- Ruler
- Hammer
- Safety goggles
- Pocket penknife

CHILD'S LADDER-BACK CHAIR CUTTING CHART

NAME OF PART	QUANTITY	DIAMETER (INCHES)	LENGTH (INCHES)	DESCRIPTION
Back legs A	2	½–¾	26	hardwood
Top seat support stretchers B	2	½–¾	11	hardwood
Front/back stretchers C	4	½–¾	10	hardwood
Top side stretchers D	2	½–¾	10	hardwood
Bottom side braces E	2	¼–½	11½	hardwood
Bottom brace F	2	½	13	hardwood
Front leg/arm G	2	½–¾	27	pliable forked
Ladder-Backs H	5	½	8–9½	hardwood
Top rung I	1	¼	12	hardwood
Boards	5	¼	2x12	box-wood or pine

DIRECTIONS

Cutting the Branches

1. Cut two ½" to ¾" diameter twigs for back legs A, each 26" long.
2. Cut two ½" to ¾" diameter twigs for top seat support stretchers B, each 11" long.

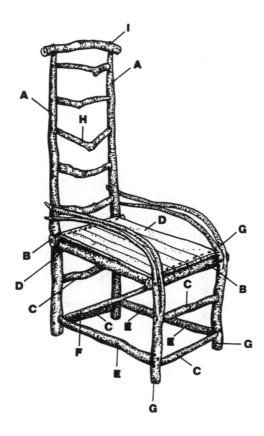

3. Cut four ½" to ¾" diameter twigs for front/back stretchers C, each 9" long.
4. Cut two ½" to ¾" diameter twigs for top side stretchers D, each 10" long.
5. Cut two ½" to ¾" diameter twigs for bottom side braces E, each 11½" long.
6. Cut two ¼" to ½" diameter twigs for bottom brace F, each 13" long.
7. Cut two ½" diameter forked twigs for front leg/arm G, each 27" long.
8. Cut five ¼" to ½" diameter twigs for ladder-backs H, each 8" to 9" long.
9. Cut one ½" diameter twig for top rung I, 12" long.

Building the Chair

1. Begin construction from the back bottom. Butt two back stretcher parts C between back legs A. Place the bottom stretcher 1" up along the back leg and position the second stretcher 4" higher. Drill a pilot hole from the outside of the leg and nail in place.
2. Add the two bottom front stretchers in the same manner.

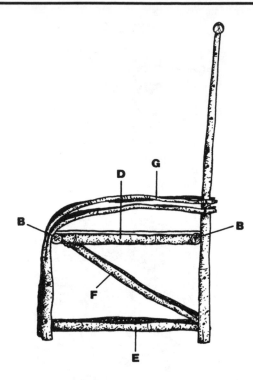

3. Overlap top stretcher B along back legs A. Drill pilot holes from the back and nail in place.
4. Repeat with front stretchers B and front legs G. Nail from the front.
5. To add the bottom side braces E, nail from the outside to the back leg and from the outside to the front leg G.

Adding the Ladder-Back
1. Butt ladder parts H from the bottom upward. Taper the ends of the twigs with a penknife as you go up the ladder.
2. With ladder parts H butted between both back legs A along the inside, drill pilot holes and nail in place from the sides of legs A.
3. Place top ladder rung I across the top of back legs A. Drill through both pieces and nail in place through the top of part I into parts A.

Forming the Arms
1. Gently bend forked legs G toward back legs A and position in place at a comfortable slant. From the side, drill pilot holes and nail in place along the outside edge of back legs A.

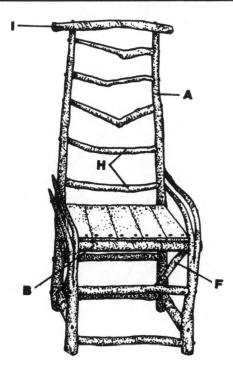

Making the Seat

1. Position the five precut seat slats along the two top stretchers B. Cut and fit to size at this point, if necessary.
2. Drill pilot holes and nail seat slats to front and back stretchers B, using two nails on the front stretcher for each board and one nail for each stretcher at the back seat boards.

Finishing

Depending on where you intend to use the chair, you may or may not decide to paint it. Painted white or pink and fitted with a chintz cushion, it serves as a charming accent to a young girl's room. To keep its natural look, leave the chair as is and paint the seat with a wash of blue or green to add an heirloom look.

S L A B - T O P   S T O O L

This easy-to-master technique turns an ordinary slab of wood into a useful piece of furniture. The twig-legged ledge is the perfect resting place for tired feet, a cup of tea or a potted plant. With a little imagination, slabs or planks in various sizes, and forked twigs you can create a variety of original pieces. A hand saw, drill, slice of wood and three multi-forked twigs make up the basic design.

MATERIALS

Select forked, multi-forked and pliable branches of willow, alder, cedar, or another similar wood for the legs. It is important to have pliable green branches for the slight bending required to create the legs. 16" lengths with diameters from ¾" to 1" are used in the stool pictured here. You will also need a log slice, 3" thick and

12" in diameter. Note: Log slices can be obtained from a logger, tree-trimmer or firewood supplier. Thick planks of wood from the lumber yard also work well.

T O O L S

- ◆ Cross cut hand saw
- ◆ Clippers or garden shears
- ◆ Ruler or measuring tape
- ◆ Marking pencil
- ◆ ⅜" varible-speed drill with a selection of bits
- ◆ Sandpaper (or electric sander)
- ◆ Safety goggles
- ◆ Work gloves

LEGS

S L A B - T O P   S T O O L   C U T T I N G   C H A R T

NAME OF PART	QUANTITY	DIAMETER (INCHES)	LENGTH (INCHES)	DESCRIPTION
Legs	3	¾–1	16	multi–forked and pliable
Stool top	1	12	3"thick	seasoned wood, such as pine, maple, oak or cherry

D I R E C T I O N S

1. Cut three multi-forked ¾" to 1" diameter branches for the legs, each 16" long. This length allows for trimming. Note: The height of the completed stool is 16".
2. Prepare the 2"-diameter wood slab by sanding the surfaces smooth before the legs are installed.
3. Lay the slab-top face down on a worktable. Arrange the legs, using the leg-placement diagram as a guide. Keep in mind for the overall design that every twig is unique.
4. Using a pencil, mark the slab at the points where the legs will be inserted.
5. Note: Holes should be slightly smaller than the twig to allow for a snug fit. Drill holes for one leg at a time approximately 1" deep at the pencilmarks. Bend slightly and adjust the legs as necessary to guarantee a level piece.
7. Taper, drill and fit the remaining two legs. Make sure the piece stands straight as you proceed.
8. Stand stool upright and trim the bottoms of legs if necessary.

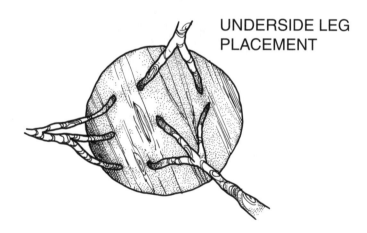

UNDERSIDE LEG PLACEMENT

Finishing

Left unadorned this piece stands on its own as a utilitarian work of art, and does not require paint, stain or varnish. Like all twig pieces, however, individual taste and space dictate finishing techniques. You may choose to add a plump cushion, or upholster the top in the same fashion as the Vanity Chair.

LAMP TABLE

This table's square top and graceful proportions make it especially suitable to hold a bedside reading lamp. The lovely coloring of its forked and gnarled parts seems particularly striking in almost any room. To speed up construction you may choose to forego the branch top and add a level top made of pine slats or painted plywood. This would give you a smooth surface on which to rest a drink or place a lamp. For optimum comfort, you may decide to adjust the height so that it is the same as your sofa or bed.

MATERIALS

Use willow, cedar, or any pliable branches. Lengths will range from 19" to 60" and from ¾" to 1½" in diameter for the table legs and rims. Four forked branches (any hardwood), 20" long and 1" in diameter, will be needed for the stretchers. Twenty straight branches (any hardwood), 22" long and 1" in diameter, are required for the table top, or you may substitute a board for the top. You will also need galvanized flathead nails in assorted sizes (#2p, #4p, #6p, #8p, and #10p) and string to hold the bow shape while you are working with masking tape.

TOOLS

- ♦ Single bit axe for felling trees
- ♦ Crosscut hand saw
- ♦ Clippers or garden shears
- ♦ Ruler or measuring tape
- ♦ Marking pencil
- ♦ Hammer
- ♦ Drill with a selection of bits
- ♦ Safety goggles
- ♦ Work gloves
- ♦ Pocket knife (optional)
- ♦ Keyhole saw (optional)
- ♦ Drift punch (optional)

LAMP TABLE CUTTING CHART

NAME OF PART	QUANTITY	DIAMETER (INCHES)	LENGTH (INCHES)	DESCRIPTION
Legs A	4	1	60	pliable, green
Stretchers B	4	1	20	forked, hardwood
Top C	20	¾–1	22	straight, hardwood
Side rim D	2	1½	22	straight, hardwood
Front rim DD	2	1½	19	straight, hardwood
Bottom brace F	2	½	13	hardwood
Front leg/arm G	2	½–¾	27	pliable forked

DIRECTIONS

Cutting the Branches

1. Cut four 1" diameter pliable (green) branches for legs A, each 60" long.
2. Cut four 1" diameter forked branches for stretchers B, each 20" long.

3. Cut two 1½" diameter branches for side rim D, each 22" long.

4. Cut two 1½" diameter branches for front rim DD, each 19" long.

5. Cut 20 ¾" to 1" straight branches for top C, each 22" long.

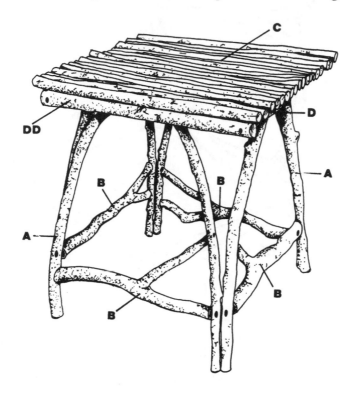

Laying Out the Sub-Assembly

1. Carefully bend leg A into a U-shaped bow. Using the string, tie the ends together to hold the shape while construction is in progress. The ends should be 20" apart.

2. Butt forked stretcher B inside of bowed leg A. Join B to A using pilot hole and nail construction.

3. Repeat steps 1 and 2 with remaining three legs A.

4. Stand all four A/B parts up. Forming a quadrangle, arrange the A/B parts for maximum contact.

5. Using two to three nails each, nail legs A together from the inside at their meeting points, using pilot hole and nail construction.

6. Stand the construction upright and check for stability. Adjust the leg bottoms, if necessary.

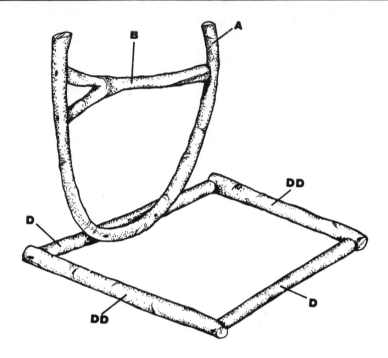

Adding the Rims

1. With the leg bottom up, place the construction on your workbench. Cut, fit, and lay side rims D and front rims DD around the outer edge of bowed leg members A. Join D and DD together at their meeting points, again using pilot hole and nail construction.

2. At the midpoints of the bows, using two nails each, join the arched tops of legs A to the inside of the D/DD framework, using pilot hole and nail construction.

Adding the Top

1. Stand the table upright. Lay out top C, resting the pieces on rims DD and D. Adjust the pieces to provide as flat a surface as possible.

2. Using masking tape, tape all top branches C together. With the top side down, place taped table top C on the workbench. With the bottom facing up, place the top of the leg/rim construction on top of the taped C part.

3. Drill and nail each top C piece to rims D and DD. Select a nail long enough to go through the rim branch a short way into C, but short enough to avoid pushing the nail through the top.

Finishing

Left natural or painted, this table can adapt to the mood of many rooms. With painted furniture so popular today, you may decide to indulge your passion for personal style by painting it a combination of colors. If you opted to build the table with a plywood top, you might paint the top and leave the legs natural for a sophisticated mix of twig and paint.

FLOOR LAMP

Here is an easy-to-make beginner's project that will help infuse your home with personality. Good lighting adds character and comfort to a room; you will want to build several of these to provide inviting illumination and interesting style. Twigs with crooks and bends are put to good use here in order to permit the legs to splay outward. Build shorter versions for popular table-top models.

MATERIALS

Any hardwood, such as beech, birch, or cherry ranging from 52"–58" high and 1" in diameter. Note: this lamp is 56" high. When looking for twigs in the woods, try to find twigs of similar dimensions. Keep in mind that you want to have the lamp legs splay outward, so look for branches with interesting crooks and bends at one end. You will also need a hardwood branch, 3½" tall and 1½" in diameter for the socket support spacer, as well as a selection of ¾" diameter branches at least 11" long for the stretchers. This project requires an electrical kit, available in most hardware stores, a light bulb and a lampshade.

TOOLS

- Single bit axe for felling trees
- Crosscut hand saw
- Ruler or measuring tape
- Sharp knife
- Drill
- A selection of bits for Phillips-Head drywall screws (1¼", 1⅝" and 2")
- Hammer and galvanized flathead nails (optional, to be used in place of screws)
- Plumb bob
- Pliers (optional)
- Safety goggles
- Work gloves

FLOOR LAMP CUTTING CHART

NAME OF PART	QUANTITY	DIAMETER (INCHES)	LENGTH (INCHES)	DESCRIPTION
Legs A	3	¾ to 1	56	birch, willow or any green hardwood
Stretchers B	3	½–¾	11–14	birch or willow
Socket support C	1	1½	3½	birch, cedar, or any hardwood

DIRECTIONS

Cutting the Branches

1. Cut three 1" diameter branches, each 56" long for the lamp legs A.

Note: It is a good idea to use slightly tapered branches, with a bottom diameter of 1" and a top of ¾". These branches must be green and pliable in order to permit slight bending.

2. Cut three branches ½" to ¾" in diameter and 11" to 14" long for the stretchers B.

3. Cut one 1½" diameter branch, 3½" long for the socket-support spacer C.

Building the Lamp

1. Mark the center of the 1½" diameter socket-support spacer C. Drill a hole completely through the socket-support at the center mark, wide enough to accommodate the lamp nipple that comes in the electrical kit.

2. Screw the nipple in place, using the pliers if needed. Check the hole to make certain it is clear all the way through to permit the wire to be installed. Set the socket-support aside.

Attaching the Legs to the Socket-support

1. Check each of the three legs to be sure they will fit tightly against the socket-support. Use a sharp knife to shave off any interference.

2. Note: Drill pilot holes will be drilled at an angle as not to interfere with the future wiring. Mark a point from the top of a leg A, 1½" down, and then a second point at approximately 2" down from the first. Butt leg securely against socket-support C, leaving 1" to extend beyond part C. Hold leg firmly in place and drill at an angle, at the two premarked locations, through the leg and part way through the socket-support.

3. Using the correct Phillips-Head Drywall screw (or the galvanized nails), attach leg A to socket-support C.
4. Repeat the above steps with the remaining two legs.

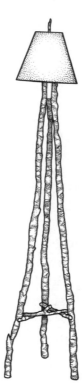

Adding the Stretchers

Note: If you are lucky enough to have crooks and bends located at a point 8" to 12" from the bottom of the legs, you will want to attach the stretchers at this point. Permit the wood to dictate the design. The stretchers B will be attached under and over each another, forming an equilateral triangle.

1. Drill a pilot hole approximately 1" to 1½" from the end of one stretcher B and through a point 8" to 12" up from the bottom of one leg. Using Phillips-Head screws attach the stretcher to the leg at this point.
2. Gently extend the second leg outward; attach the stretcher to the extended leg in the same manner as in the preceding step.
3. To attach the second stretcher B place one end of the second stretcher over the installed stretcher and using pilot hole construction attach to the same leg.

4. Attach the third stretcher over one installed stretcher and under the other.

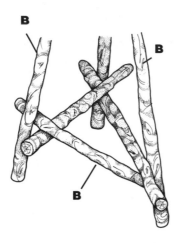

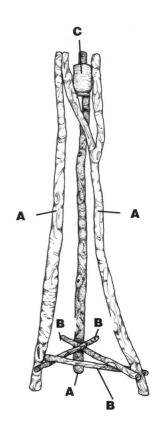

Leveling and Adding Electrical Components
Stand the lamp upright. Thread the plumb bob through the lamp nipple and suspend the line to check if the lamp stands straight. Use a sharp knife to adjust the ends, if necessary. Add the electrical parts according to the directions on the purchased kit.

Finishing
Chalk white, matte black or metallic gold paint can dramatically change the look of this lamp but nothing will alter its appearance as much as the lampshade you choose. A pale gray linen shade adds a soft glow; an opaque paper shade adds drama. Try a basket turned upside-down or the grapevine lampshade on page 236 for texture and an illusion of softness when the light shines through.

THREE-SECTION
FOLDING SCREEN

This basic screen design can be adjusted to any size. The three-foot-high screen shown here makes a charming summer fireplace screen or a camouflage for an unsightly radiator. Building a taller screen requires a great deal of patience. The bottom branches often need trimming as the wood shrinks and dries. It is a good idea to begin with the smaller size screen.

Choose a hardwood such as willow, birch, beech, or cherry. Lengths will range from 15" to 36". The branches should be 1" in diameter. You will also require galvanized flathead nails in assorted sizes (#2p, #4p, and #6p) and heavy gauge wire.

TOOLS

- Single bit axe for felling trees
- Crosscut hand saw
- Clippers or garden shears
- Ruler or measuring tape
- Marking pencil
- Drill with a selection of bits
- Hammer
- Wire clippers and pliers
- Safety goggles
- Work gloves

THREE-SECTION SCREEN CUTTING CHART

NAME OF PART	QUANTITY	DIAMETER (INCHES)	LENGTH (INCHES)	DESCRIPTION
Vertical supports A	6	1	36	hardwood
Horizontal braces B	6	1	15	hardwood

DIRECTIONS

Cutting the Branches

1. Cut six 1" diameter branches for vertical supports A, each 36" long.
2. Cut six 1" diameter branches for horizontal braces B, each 15" long.

Assembling the Panels

1. With the front side up, place two vertical supports A approximately 11" apart on the worktable.
2. Overlap the first horizontal brace B across the two branches A, 9" from the bottom. Drill and nail in place. The braces should extend 1" on either side of the supports. Place the second horizontal brace B across the two branches A, 4" from the top. Drill pilot holes and nail in place from the front of the horizontal braces B.

3. Repeat with two more A branches and two more B branches.

4. Position the two completed panels face up on the worktable, one on the left and the other on the right. These are the end panels. Lay the two remaining vertical supports A in the center. Arrange the top and bottom horizontal braces B across the vertical supports so that their top ends overlap the already completed braces of the other two end panels. The center panel will be attached to the end panels at this meeting point. Complete the center panel by joining the horizontal braces B to the vertical supports A, as in step 2 above, being certain that the center horizontal braces are positioned just above the adjoining end horizontal braces.

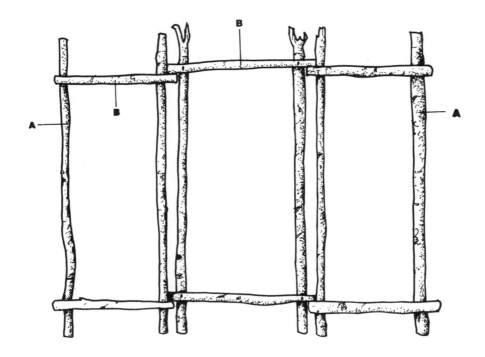

Joining the Panels

1. Overlap center panel horizontal braces B above side panel horizontal braces B. Drill a hole completely through both braces, from the top to the bottom. Repeat with the other side panel.

2. Thread 6" of wire through the horizontal brace holes. Using pliers, tighten the wire on the backside so it is out of sight.

Finishing

The inside of the panels need to be filled. There are several options depending on the mood you want to create. For a romantic look, tack a rose-strewn chintz to the inside framework, or tie lacy ribbons across the opening from the top to bottom horizontal braces. To create an updated country look, stencil a cheerful motif on white cotton duck, tack it inside the framework, and wrap grapevine between the vertical supports so that both supports are joined by the vine. To link the screen to its surroundings, try tacking a few yards of matching wallpaper over the open panels.

INDOOR SHUTTERS

These easy-to-make indoor shutters can be accommodated to most interior windows. With their rustic charm, they may be just the window covering needed to add a breath of nature to your room.

MATERIALS

Purchase one pair of interior, fabric-insert shutters according to your window size. You will also need an assortment of twigs whose diameters and lengths will be determined by the size of the shutter opening. You will also need contact cement or a heavy-duty commercial glue. A glue gun and super strength wood glue may be used.

TOOLS

- ◆ Garden shears or clippers
- ◆ Pencil
- ◆ Ruler or tape measure

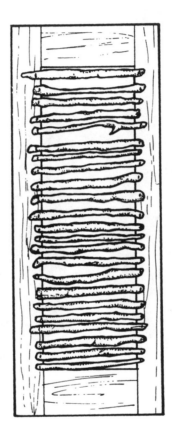

DIRECTIONS

1. If your shutters require sanding, staining, or painting, complete any such finishing work before the twigs are applied.
2. Lay the finished shutter panels face down on a worktable. Measure the back opening. This measurement will be slightly larger than the actual front opening. The twigs will be inserted so they rest on the inside. Using a pencil, mark the twigs to the same dimensions as the shutter opening.

3. Using the garden shears, cut the twigs at the pencil markings.

4. When you have a sufficient number of cut twigs, apply the glue to the inside of the shutter opening, one section at a time. Press twigs into place in even rows until the entire opening is filled. A few forked or crooked branches are nice, but do not use too many. The finished result should look tidy.

Finishing

Twig indoor shutters can be finished in numerous ways to accent and enhance any room. Painted pink, they add a casual note to a traditional setting. Painted dusky blue and surrounded by white woodwork, they add a crisp, country French accent. Paint them a bright turquoise and a sun-drenched Caribbean morning seems to smile into your North American cabin. Or, you may want to paint only the wooden shutters, allowing the natural beauty of the branches to filter the light.

CHAPTER 5

Household Things

PICTURE FRAME #1

W hen using white birch for this frame, try to keep its contents simple. The 14" x 18" opening, surrounded by fretwork, lends itself to a simple vintage needlepoint or a mirror.

MATERIALS

Use such woods as birch, beech, hickory, or cedar. Lengths will range from 4" to 31" and diameters from ½" to 1". You will need galvanized flathead nails in assorted sizes (#4p, #6p, #8p, and #10p) and finishing nails (¾", 1", and 1½").

TOOLS

- ♦ Single bit axe for felling trees
- ♦ Coping saw
- ♦ Crosscut hand saw
- ♦ Ruler
- ♦ Drill with a selection of bits
- ♦ Hammer
- ♦ Wood chisel
- ♦ Marking pencil
- ♦ Safety goggles
- ♦ Pocket knife (optional)
- ♦ Paint or stain of your choice (I like to use barn-red paint)

PICTURE FRAME #1 CUTTING CHART

NAME OF PART	QUANTITY	DIAMETER (INCHES)	LENGTH (INCHES)	DESCRIPTION
Frame sides A	2	1	31	hardwood
Top and bottom frame parts B	2	1	27	hardwood
Trim C	4	½	8	hardwood
Side trim CC	4	½	4	hardwood
Corner pieces D	8	½	3	hardwood

DIRECTIONS

Cutting the Branches
1. Cut two 1" diameter branches for frame sides A, each 31" long.
2. Cut two 1" diameter branches for top and bottom frame parts B, each 27" long.
3. Cut four ½" diameter branches, 8" long, for trim C, and four pieces 4" long for side trim CC.
4. Cut eight ½" diameter branches, 3" long, for corner pieces D.

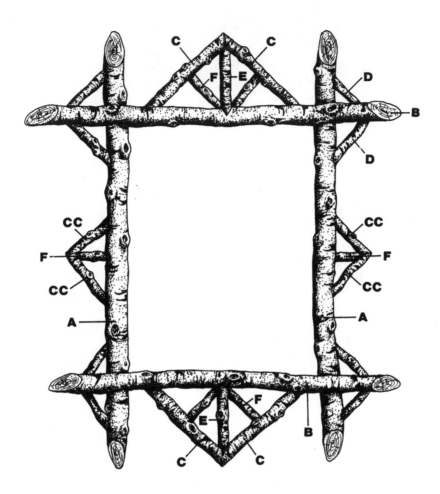

Laying Out the Main Frame
 1. Arrange the two side bars A, and top and bottom bars B, so that they frame an opening that is 15" wide and 18" long.
 2. Using a pencil, mark all branches where they cross (about 5" from the ends) in order to cut notches.

Cutting the Notches
 1. Using the crosscut hand saw, cut a notch between the pencil markings on each branch piece.

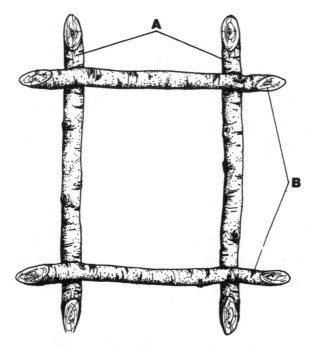

2. Using the chisel, chisel out each notch. (Note: Each notch should extend to half the diameter of the branch, so that the branches are flush when fit together.)
3. Fit pieces A and B together, adjusting the size of the notches if necessary.

Tapering the Branch Ends
1. On the front side of the four frame pieces, make a pencil mark 2" from the end of each branch on all four pieces.
2. Using the coping saw, taper each piece from the pencil mark to the ends.

Assembling the Main Frame

1. Reassemble the notched pieces with the back sides up.
2. Drill a pilot hole through one notched intersection from the back, making sure you do not penetrate more than halfway through the lower branch to prevent nail heads showing from the front.
3. Hammer a nail through the hole, choosing a nail just shorter than the thickness of the two branches. Nail from the back.
4. Repeat for the three remaining notched intersections.

Adding the Fretwork Trim

1. With the front sides facing up, lay out the fretwork branches according to the Assembly Diagram.
2. Using a pocket knife or coping saw, bevel the ends if desired.
3. Mark the places for nail placement. Select a finishing nail just long enough to go through the fretwork branch and a short way into the main frame.
4. Nail C in place, as shown in the Assembly Diagram.

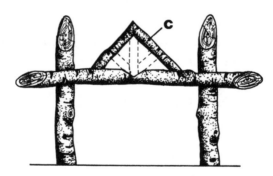

5. Nail CC in place—see diagram page 128.
6. Fill in remaining fretwork and the eight corner pieces D, drilling and nailing carefully as you go.
7. Stain or paint the tapered ends of the branches. This gives the frame a more finished, aged quality.

Finishing

The beautiful markings of birch twigs are best left natural. You can vary the look by painting the frame tips with the room's coordinating color.

PICTURE FRAME #2

This two- by two-and-a-half-foot frame is an elongated version of the preceding picture frame. Its primitive spirit helps create that down-home feeling, whether it is holding a mirror or a family portrait.

MATERIALS

Use woods such as birch, beech, hickory, or cedar, in lengths ranging from 3" to 31", ½" to 1½" in diameter. You will need galvanized flathead nails in assorted sizes (#4p, #6p, #8p, and #10p) and finishing nails (¾", 1", and 1½").

TOOLS

- ♦ Single bit axe for felling trees
- ♦ Coping saw
- ♦ Crosscut hand saw
- ♦ Ruler
- ♦ Drill with a selection of bits
- ♦ Hammer
- ♦ Wood chisel
- ♦ Marking pencil
- ♦ Safety goggles
- ♦ Pocket penknife (optional)
- ♦ Paint or stain of your choice (I like to use barn-red paint)

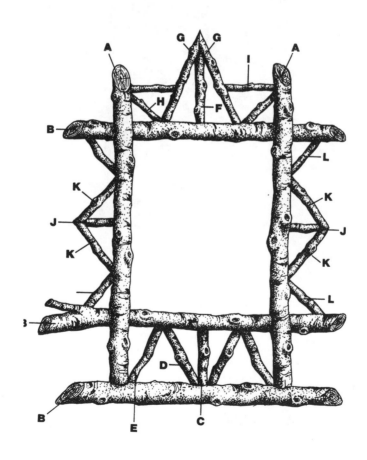

PICTURE FRAME #2 CUTTING CHART

NAME OF PART	QUANTITY	DIAMETER (INCHES)	LENGTH (INCHES)	DESCRIPTION
Frame sides A	2	1	31	hardwood
Top and bottom parts B	3	1	26½	hardwood
Fretwork twig C	1	1	5	hardwood
Fretwork twig D	2	¾	6	hardwood
Fretwork twig E	2	¾	6½	hardwood
Fretwork center bar F	1	1	7½	hardwood
Fretwork peak G	2	¾	10½	hardwood
Fretwork pieces H	2	½	3½	hardwood
Fretwork bracing branches I	2	¾	5½	hardwood
Side support fretwork J	2	½	3	hardwood
Side fretwork peaks K	4	½	6	hardwood
Side bracing branches L	4	½	4	hardwood

DIRECTIONS

Cutting the Branches

1. Cut two 1" diameter branches for frame sides A, each 31" long.
2. Cut three 1" diameter branches for top and bottom parts B, each 26½" long.
3. Cut one 1" diameter branch for fretwork twig C, 5" long.
4. Cut two ¾" diameter branches for fretwork twig D, 6" long.
5. Cut two ¾" diameter branches for fretwork twig E, 6½" long.
6. Cut one 1" diameter branch for fretwork center bar F, 7½" long.
7. Cut two ¾" diameter branches for top fretwork peak G, 10½" long.
8. Cut two ½" diameter branches for top fretwork pieces H, 3½" long.
9. Cut two ¾" diameter branches for top fretwork bracing branches I, 5½" long.
10. Cut two ½" diameter branches for side support fretwork J, 3" long.
11. Cut four ½" diameter branches for side fretwork peaks K, 6" long.
12. Cut four ½" diameter branches for side bracing branches L, 4" long.

Laying Out the Main Frame

1. Arrange the two side bars A, and two of the top and bottom bars B, so that they frame an opening that measures 13½" wide and 16½" long.
2. Using a pencil, mark all branches where they cross (about 5" from the ends).

Cutting the Notches

1. Using the crosscut hand saw, cut a notch between the pencil markings halfway into each branch.
2. Using the chisel, chisel out each notch. (Note: Each notch should extend only as half as deep as the diameter of the branch, so that the branches are flush when fit together.)
3. Fit pieces A and B together, adjusting the size of the notches if necessary.

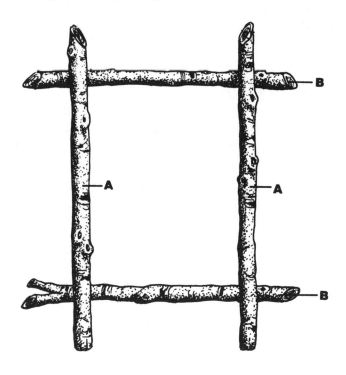

Tapering the Branch Ends

1. Choose one side of the frame to be the front. Place the frame front side up on a worktable.
2. Center and butt lower bar B (the unnotched piece) against the two exposed side bars A (see the Assembly Diagram).

3. On the front side of the five framing pieces, make a pencil mark 2" from each end on the eight exposed branch ends.
4. Disassemble the frame. Using the coping saw, taper each piece from the pencil mark to the end.

Assembling the Main Frame
1. Reassemble the main frame (notched pieces) with the back side facing up.
2. Drill a pilot hole through one notched intersection from the back, making sure you do not penetrate more than halfway through the lower branch to prevent nail heads showing from the front.
3. Hammer a nail through the hole, choosing one just shorter than the combined thickness of the two branches. Remember, you should be nailing from the back.
4. Repeat for the three remaining notched intersections.
5. Reposition the lower bar (remaining unnotched piece B), butting it against the bottom of both A pieces as shown in the Assembly Diagram.
6. Drill a pilot hole through lower bar B into the ends of each side bar A, and hammer a nail into each hole.

Fitting and Laying Out the Lower Fretwork
1. Place the frame, front side up, on a worktable. Refer to the Assembly Diagram, and lay out fretwork twigs C, D, and E, bevelling the ends with the coping saw (or pocket penknife) as required.

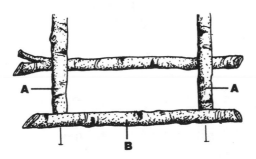

2. For each piece of fretwork, select a finishing nail just long enough to go through the adjacent bar and three-quarters of the way into the fretwork twig.

3. Mark the spot where the pieces are to be nailed by placing a pencil dot on the bar and on the fretwork twig.

4. Stand the frame upright; hold center piece C in place. Drill a pilot hole through upper bar B into C, and nail in place. Turn the frame over and drill another pilot hole. Nail through lower bar B into C.

5. In the same manner, attach D and E.

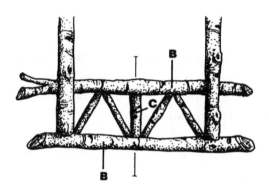

Fitting and Laying Out the Upper Fretwork

1. Refer to the Assembly Diagram and lay out the twigs F, G, H, and I. Mark the pieces for nail placement as in step 3 above.

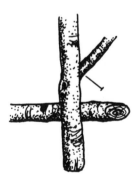

2. Begin with center piece F. Drill and nail in place, as with twig C. Now fit in diagonal twigs G and H. Drill a pilot hole and nail up through the top bar into the bottoms of the twigs.

3. Fit horizontal pieces I between diagonal twigs G and side piece A. Drill pilot holes and nail them parallel to top piece B and at a 90° angle to side piece A. Fit, drill pilot holes, and nail diagonal pieces H at a 45° angle between side pieces A and top piece B.

Fitting and Laying Out Side Fretwork

1. Refer to the Assembly Diagram. Fit and lay out fretwork pieces J, K, and L at the sides of the frame, bevelling as required. Mark the pieces with a pencil dot for nail placement.
2. Working from the center, attach twig J at a 90° angle to side bar A. Attach twigs K at about a 45° angle between twig J and side bar A and twigs L at about a 45° angle between side bars A and bar B to each side of the frame, drilling pilot holes and nailing as you go. Repeat for the opposite side.
3. Stain or paint the tapered ends of the branches.

Finishing

Coordinating a colored mat with the painted tips of the frame will add a unique and bright touch to any room.

TABLE-TOP
PICTURE FRAME

At home or at work, this tabletop frame is the perfect way to display one 8" x 10" photo (or two back-to-back) between two ⅛" thick panes of polished-edge glass. Its simple clean lines are clever and contemporary—it's natural bark, rustic and primitive. At home in any setting, you will want to make several in different sizes for your favorite photos.

MATERIALS

You will need one 1½" diameter birch pole, and one 2" diameter birch pole; both approximately two feet long. *This longer length is required for ease in cutting the grooves.* You will also need four 1¼" Phillips-head dry wall screws (or 1¼" galvanized roofing nails). Two ⅛" thick, polished edge panes of glass, 8" x 10" are required along with the optional 8" x 10" picture mat.

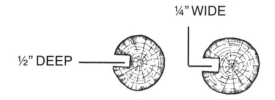

¼" WIDE

½" DEEP

T O O L S

- ◆ Single bit axe for felling trees
- ◆ Table saw
- ◆ Crosscut hand saw
- ◆ Ruler or measuring tape
- ◆ Marking pencil
- ◆ Sandpaper
- ◆ Brace and expansion bit
- ◆ Gouge or crooked knife (optional)
- ◆ Phillips-Head screwdriver (or ⅜" variable-speed drill with bit)
- ◆ Hammer (optional)
- ◆ Safety goggles
- ◆ Work gloves

D I R E C T I O N S

A table saw is required in order to make the ¼" wide, ½" deep cuts. If your workshop does not include a radial or table saw, many lumber yards or local woodworking shops are often willing to help out cutting the grooves. These woodworking shops often have an adjustable feature on their industrial table saws that allow a cutter bit to dial a selection of widths, thus permitting a one-step cutting process. *Note: For safe handling the grooves are cut in the long length, and later cut to size.*

To begin cutting the grooves, attach a square block of wood to one end of the 2" diameter pole to help keep the pole steady as it goes through the blade. With most table saws you will have to repeat the cutting process two or three times in order to achieve the ¼" wide cut.

1. Split the 2" diameter pole in half lengthwise. The pole will be cut to the correct length ofter the groove is cut. Sand the bottom (split side) to insure a flat base.
2. Cut a 13" long groove, ¼" wide and ½" deep in the 2" diameter pole.
3. Cut the split pole approximately 13" long, allowing at least 3" to extend on both sides of the cut groove.
4. Cut the same size groove ¼" wide and ½" deep) 16" long in the 1½" diameter pole.
5. Cut the 1½" diameter pole in two equal lengths, approximately 8" each.
6. Place the base down on a work surface. Position and mark the diameters of both 8" poles on top of the base approximately 2" from end.
7. Using the brace and expansion bit, hollow out both points approximately ½". For a snug fit, use a gouge or crooked knife if needed.

Assembly

Make sure the hollowed-out openings in the base are sufficient for a tight fit. Arrange one 8" pole upright in the hollow gouge facing inward, and hold it in place with one hand while drilling two pilot holes through the bottom of the base through the pole. Using the Phillips-Head screws (or roofing nails) attach the two pieces. Repeat with the remaining 8" pole. Slide two pieces of ⅛" polished-edge glass in place and slip one or two photos between the panes of glass.

CLOCK

An inexpensive clock mechanism, birch bark and mitered twigs make this handsome hexagonal timepiece. With a few simple hand tools, you can create this unique and useful project, its natural beauty elegant enough for a fine parlor or simple cabin.

MATERIALS

You will need a 9" square of white paper birch bark taken from a recently fallen tree (do not peel bark from a living tree; it will cause the tree to die). Also required are twelve straight branches of willow, alder, cedar, or another similar wood, 6" long and ¾" in diameter, as well as four straight twigs, 1½" long and ¼" in diameter for the time positions. A 5" x 8" piece of scrap lumber ¼-inch thick is needed for the back of the bark to secure the clock mechanism. Keep on hand: carpet tacks or heavy-duty staples; epoxy glue or glue sticks; ¾" and 1" finishing nails; screw-eye and leather lace for hanging (optional).

TOOLS

- Quartz clock movement and hands (available at craft stores)
- One AA battery
- Crosscut hand saw
- Scissors
- Ruler or measuring tape
- Marking pencil
- Drill with a selection of bits
- Hammer
- Staple gun (optional)
- Glue gun (optional)
- Miter box
- Safety goggles
- Work gloves

DIRECTIONS

Cutting and Mitering the Branches

You will be making two twig frames, each composed of six branches. The bark clock face is sandwiched between the two frames during the construction.

1. Using the miter box, cut twelve ¾" diameter branches for clock frame, each 5" long on outer edges with 60-degree angles in opposite directions on each end; see diagram on page 144.

Laying Out the Clock Frame

1. Place the six frame parts facedown on a worktable; assemble to form a hexagon. Butt the mitered cut ends together. At the points where they meet, drill pilot holes and using the finishing nails, nail in place.
2. Repeat the preceding step with the remaining six mitered twigs.

Making the Bark Clock Face

Note: Bark taken from freshly cut trees is generally pliable enough to use within a day or two of cutting. If you have to wait several days before you begin your project, press the bark between heavy books until you're ready to use it. To peel the bark, see page 211.

1. Place bark face down on work table. Using the pencil, trace the outline of the frame on the bark.
2. Cut bark with scissors, adjusting the size so the bark is caught securely between the twig frames.
3. Lay one frame facedown on the work surface. Place the bark facedown on top and fasten to the frame with the staples or carpet tacks.
4. Arrange the second frame on top and attach with 1" finishing nails.

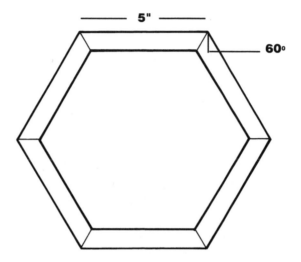

Adding the Clock Works and Clock Hands
1. Trim the scrap wood, if necessary, to fit on the back of the clock inside the back frame.
2. Using the epoxy glue (or the glue stick and glue-gun) attach the scrap wood to the back. Allow glue to dry several hours.
3. Measure and mark the center of the clock face; drill a hole through the bark face and the scrap wood back. Insert the clock mechanism according to the package directions.
4. Glue 1½" long twigs to the clock face at 12, 3, 6, and 9 positions, as shown in the photograph.
5. Add battery to clock works.

Place screw-eye at the top of the back of clock and tie leather lace in place for hanging, if desired. May also rest on a shelf or sit on a small table-top easel.

BASKET PLANTER

This 9" x 15" basket can be made in a variety of other sizes to accommodate almost any type of item. Once you master the simple construction technique, make these to give as gifts filled with an array of homemade sweets, herbs, or plants. They look charming when placed together, in varying sizes, on a mantel or sideboard.

MATERIALS

You will need 22 twigs of any wood, ranging in length from 9" to 15" and in diameter from ½" to ¾", for the basket. You will also need two branches, such as willow or alder, each 30" long and ½" to ¾" in diameter for the handle and the binding; two straight wires, 25" to 30" long; and finishing nails.

145

TOOLS

- Crosscut hand saw
- Wire cutters
- Pocket penknife (or garden shears)
- Rubber mallet
- Drill and bit
- Ruler
- Pencil
- Hammer
- Safety goggles

BASKET PLANTER CUTTING CHART

NAME OF PART	QUANTITY	DIAMETER (INCHES)	LENGTH (INCHES)	DESCRIPTION
Bottom and side basket parts A	14	½–¾	15	hardwood
End basket parts B	8	½–¾	9	hardwood
Fretwork twig C	1	½–¾	30	pliable
Binding D	1	½	30	pliable split in half lengthwise

DIRECTIONS

Cutting the Branches
1. Cut 14 twigs, ½" to ¾" in diameter, for bottom and side basket parts A, each 15" long.
2. Cut eight twigs, ½" to ¾" inches in diameter, for end basket parts B, each 9" long.
3. Cut one willow twig, approximately ¾" in diameter, for handle C, 30" long.
4. Cut one willow twig, approximately ½" in diameter 30" long for the binding, and split it in half lengthwise.

Building the Basket Bottom

1. With a pencil, mark one inch from both ends of all twigs A and B.
2. Set two end staves B aside. Drill a hole through each of the remaining 40 pencil marks, being sure that the diameter of the hole is large enough to thread your wire through.
3. After all holes are drilled, assemble eight bottom parts A on a worktable. Thread the two wires through all 16 holes, centered and evenly spaced from the ends of the wires.
4. Bend the four extended wires upward, forming a U-shape at each end of the basket.

Building the Basket Sides

1. The main basket body is built by alternatively threading side staves A and end staves B.
2. Begin by threading both ends of an end stave B, on opposite ends of one of the U-shaped wires, pushing down until it sits across the bottom staves.
3. Repeat with the other side.
4. Thread a side stave A, at a right angle to end staves B, onto the two separate wires at each end of the basket.
5. Continue layering in this fashion until the basket is one end stave short of the desired height.

Completing the Basket Sides

1. Press down all threaded staves so that they are as close to one another as possible.
2. Drill halfway into the last pair of end staves B.
3. Using wire clippers, clip the wire ends so that they fit through the holes in the tops of the end staves.
4. Using the rubber mallet, carefully drive the wire ends into the top end stave holes, thus capping off your basket. The wire ends should not protrude through the two end staves.

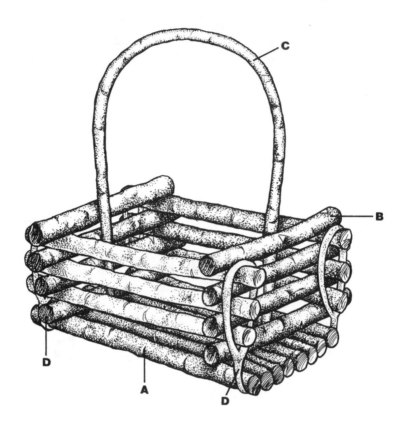

Making the Handle and Binding

1. Gently bend the willow handle into a U-shape.
2. Center it inside the basket, at each end, against the end staves.
3. Drill and nail in place from the inside, at two points where the handle meets the end staves on each side.

Wrapping and Trimming

1. To complete your basket, take one split willow shoot D and wrap it around the bottom of the bottom staves, bringing it up on the outside of the side staves and overlapping corner joints. Gently bend the willow shoot over the top side stave.
2. Using a pocket penknife (or garden shears), trim the split shoot so that it can be tucked in to touch itself at the corner of the bottom of the first overlapping joint.

Finishing

The basket planter can take on a personality of its own, depending on your choice of finishing. Painted white, its crisp lines can be softened with wild flowers and grasses. Shiny black paint evokes contemporary sophistication. You may want to try purple for unexpected panache or the familiar blue of your grandmother's china for a lovely accent. Do not be afraid of color. This small basket is a perfect opportunity to experiment and have some fun.

HORSESHOE TRIM BASKET

This petite basket, adapted from an antique design, heads the list of country charm items. Crown the handle with a fat red ribbon and fill with evergreens for a winter display. Or, tuck a lace-edged linen napkin inside before adding chocolate-covered strawberries for a springtime flavor.

MATERIALS

You will need willow, or another pliable wood, in lengths from 6" to 42" and in diameters from ¼" to ½", along with finishing nails.

TOOLS

- Garden shears or clippers
- Ruler
- Pencil
- Drill with bit (optional)

HORSESHOE TRIM BASKET CUTTING CHART

NAME OF PART	QUANTITY	DIAMETER (INCHES)	LENGTH (INCHES)	DESCRIPTION
Front and back bottom staves A	2	½	7	pliable/or hardwood
Front and back top staves B	2	½	12	pliable/or hardwood
Side and bottom staves C	8	½	4½	pliable/or hardwood
Front and back center staves D	4	½	5½	pliable/or hardwood
Handle support staves E	2	½	4½	pliable/or hardwood
Horseshoe trim F	6	¼	15½	pliable
Handles G	2	¼	42	pliable

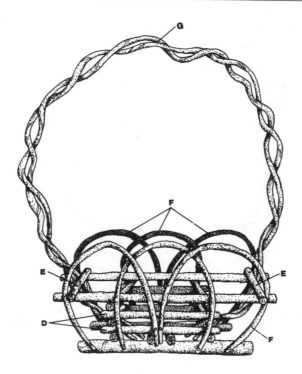

DIRECTIONS

Cutting the Branches
1. Refer to the Cutting Chart and Assembly Diagram.
2. Cut two ½" diameter branches for front and back bottom staves A, each 7" long.
3. Cut two ½" diameter branches for front and back top staves B, each 12" long.
4. Cut eight ½" diameter branches for side and bottom staves C, each 4½" long.
5. Cut four ½" diameter branches for front and back center staves D, each 5½" long.
6. Cut two ½" diameter branches for handle support staves E, each 4½" long.
7. Cut six ¼" diameter branches for horseshoe trim F, each 15½" long.
8. Cut two ¼" diameter branches for handles G, each 42" long.

Building the Basket Bottom
1. On a worktable, lay out the two bottom staves A, approximately 3" apart. Note: All parts C should extend slightly beyond parts A, B, and D so that the horseshoe trim can rest against them.
2. Lay one side bottom branch C at a right angle across one bottom stave A, 1½" from the end, being sure to extend C slightly beyond A. Nail in place.
3. Repeat with opposite end.
4. Approximately 3" from each end of bottom staves A, center two staves C across both bottom staves A. Nail in place.

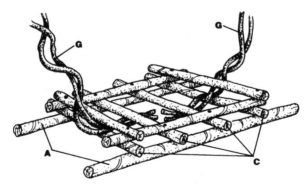

Building the Basket
1. The main basket is built by alternating staves C and staves D in a log-building manner. Staves D should parallel the bottom staves A.

2. Begin by laying one stave D across the four bottom side staves C. Nail in place, being sure to use very thin finishing nails.
3. Repeat on opposite side.
4. Lay one stave C across the ends of two parallel staves D. Nail in place.
5. Repeat on opposite side.
6. Repeat above procedure until all four staves D and remaining four staves C are used.
7. Center the two 12" staves B across the tops of the last staves C. Nail in place.
8. Rest one handle support stave E across the two top staves B, approximately 1" from the ends of B. Nail in place.
9. Repeat step 8 on the other side.

Horseshoe Trim and Handle
1. Gently bend one horseshoe twig F. Place one end of F against the outside of bottom stave C and bring it up along the other two. Drill and nail F where it meets with A and B, arching it over and bringing it down along the staves C on the opposite side. Drill and nail in place where it meets A and B. This is the center horseshoe.
2. Repeat on the opposite side of the basket.
3. Using the same method as above, nail the remaining horseshoes in place. Nailing from the front ends of bottom staves A, around handle support staves E, in front of center horseshoe trim E, and finally meeting in the middle.
4. To make the handle, take one end of handle G and tuck it between two bottom side staves C, resting it under the closest middle stave C. Gently bring it up and around to form the handle. Tuck in the other side in the same manner. Nail in place at several meeting points (see diagram).
5. Repeat with the remaining handle, carefully wrapping it around the first handle.

Finishing
The color you choose to paint your basket has the power make it either subtle or sensational. Select a soft pastel or vivid bright but stay away from muddy colors. Try bright orange as an accent color or a washed teal for subtle harmony.

PLANT STANDARD

The sturdy tripod base is a good foundation for this playful natural willow form with its crowns of branches. The *standard*, unlike the more familiar trellis, is a plant support that stands on its own and does not require a wall to lean on. You will want to make several of these in smaller sizes to fit into standard-size nursery pots. They look lovely indoors covered with trailing ivy and anchored with clematis in the garden.

MATERIALS

The plant standard pictured here is 68" high and was built for pole beans in the vegetable garden. Collect three pliable twigs, such as alder, willow, hazel or mad-

154

rone, ranging from 58" to 68" in length, with diameters of 1" to 2" tapering to approximately ¼" to ½". Select forked twigs for this project, standing each one upright as you go along to determine its ability to splay out at the bottom. You will also need one hardwood branch, 5" long and 1½" to 2" in diameter, as well as assorted straight twigs 7" to 13" long and ½" in diameter. Galvanized flathead nails (#2p, #4p and #6p) fasten the twigs together.

T O O L S

- ♦ Crosscut hand saw
- ♦ Garden shears or clippers
- ♦ Drill with a selection of bits
- ♦ Pencil
- ♦ Ruler
- ♦ Hammer
- ♦ Sharp pocket knife (optional)
- ♦ Safety goggles
- ♦ Work gloves

P L A N T   S T A N D A R D   C U T T I N G   C H A R T

NAME OF PART	QUANTITY	DIAMETER (INCHES)	LENGTH (INCHES)	DESCRIPTION
Legs A	3	1–2	58–68	pliable forked
Center space B	1	1½–2	5	hardwood
Bottom stretchers C	3	½	7	hardwood
Top stretchers D	3	½	13	forked

D I R E C T I O N S

Cutting the Branches
1. Cut three 1" to 2" diameter pliable forked twigs for the legs A, each 58" to 8" long.
2. Cut one 1½" to 2" diameter hardwood branch for the center spacer B, 5" long.

3. Cut three ½" diameter twigs for the bottom stretchers C, each 7" long.
4. Cut three ½" diameter forked twigs for the top stretchers D, each 13" long.

Building the Plant Standard

1. Begin construction by attaching the legs A, to the center spacer B. Located a point approximately 26" from the bottom end of one leg, preferably at a natural bend of the twig, to attach the center spacer.
2. Butt the center spacer against one leg; using the pencil, mark two points 3" apart to join the leg to part B. Drill pilot holes and nail in place.
3. Repeat with the remaining two legs A.

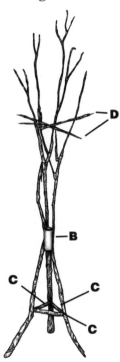

Adding the Bottom Stretchers

1. Place the construction on a worktable. On the inside of each leg A, make a pencil mark 8" from the bottom.
2. Taper the ends of the bottom stretchers C with a sharp pocket knife or garden shears.
3. Butt each stretcher C to the leg A against which it will be nailed, checking for a tight fit.

4. Drill pilot holes through the ends of stretcher C into two legs A at the pencil marks. Join C to A, lining up the pilot holes and nailing three-quarters of the way through. Note: Leave one-quarter of the driven nail exposed until the standard is assembled. This prevents the driven nails from being loosened as you proceed.
5. Repeat from Step 4, fitting, drilling and nailing the remaining two stretchers C to the two legs A, forming an equilateral triangle. Make sure your construction stands straight and even as you proceed. Using a sharp pocket knife, or hand saw, trim the legs as necessary to guarantee a straight stand.

Adding the Top Stretchers

1. The flexibility of the branches and your personal sense of design will determine the points where the top stretchers are added. Gently move the extending twig crowns, separating them to add balance to the structure and to accommodate the top stretchers D.
2. Using pilot hole and nail construction, add the top stretchers D to the tops of the forked legs A at locations that will balance your piece. The photograph is a guide; but be willing to let the materials guide you.

STANDING PLANTER

This planter is 9" deep and 32" wide to accommodate a standard flower box insert. Its height (built here to 34") can be adjusted to fit any location. The decorative forked branch braces help strengthen the piece with ingenuity. With its sculptural design, the standing planter makes an appealing foundation for a collection of houseplants, joining art with function.

MATERIALS

Use such woods as birch, beech, cedar, or willow. Lengths will range from 9" to 36" with diameters from ¼" to 1". You will also need willow, or a similar pliable wood, ¼" in diameter and 36" in length for decorative trim. Galvanized flathead nails in assorted sizes (#4p, #6p, and #8p) and finishing nails (¾" and 1") will also be required.

TOOLS

- Single bit axe for felling trees
- Crosscut hand saw
- Clippers or garden shears
- Ruler or measuring tape
- Marking pencil
- Drill with a selection of bits
- Hammer
- Safety goggles
- Work gloves
- Pocket knife (optional)

STANDING PLANTER CUTTING CHART

NAME OF PART	QUANTITY	DIAMETER (INCHES)	LENGTH (INCHES)	DESCRIPTION
Legs A	4	1	34	straight
Beams B	6	¾	32	straight
Side rails C	8	¾	9	straight
Plant box supports D	4	¾	9	straight
Front and back braces E	2	¼	32	forked
Trim F (side)	2	¼	30	pliable
Trim F (front/back)	2	¼	50	pliable
Decorative trim	1	¼	36	pliable

DIRECTIONS

Cutting the Branches

1. Cut four 1" diameter branches for legs A, each 34" long.
2. Cut six ¾" diameter branches for beams B, each 32" long.
3. Cut eight ¾" diameter branches for side rails C, each 9" long.
4. Cut four ¾" diameter branches for plant box supports D, each 9" long.
5. Cut two ¼" diameter forked branches for front and back braces E, each 32" long.

6. Cut four ¼" diameter pliable branches for trim F, two 30" long and two 50" long.
7. Cut one ¼" diameter decorative trim, 36" long.

Laying Out the Sub-Assembly
1. Using a pencil and ruler, mark the 12 points where beams B will be joined to the four legs A to form the front and back of the planter. The top beam should be placed 2" from the top of each leg. The second beam is then placed 6" below the top beam. Place the bottom beam 21" below the second beam.
2. Drill pilot holes from the sides of the legs into the ends of the beams. Nail in place from the outsides of the legs using #4p nails.

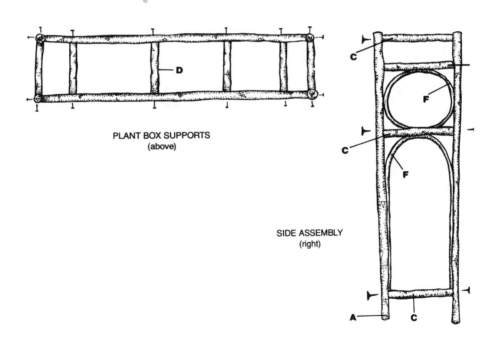

PLANT BOX SUPPORTS
(above)

SIDE ASSEMBLY
(right)

Connecting the Sides
1. Using a pencil and ruler, mark the four locations on each leg where side rails C will be placed. Starting from the top, position the first rail as close to the top of each leg as possible. The second rail should then be

placed 2" lower. Place the third rail another 6" lower, and position the bottom rail 21" below the third rail.

2. Drill pilot holes from the sides of the legs into the side rails, and nail in place using #4p nails.

Adding the Plant Box Supports
1. Using a pencil and ruler, mark equally spaced points where box supports D will be joined to the front and back beams. Drill pilot holes and nail in place using #4p nails.

Adding the Front and Back Forked Braces
1. From the inside corner of one back leg, place forked branch E at a pleasing angle and nail in place using a finishing nail. Drive a nail where the forked branches meet the top and middle beam as well. Repeat on the front side.

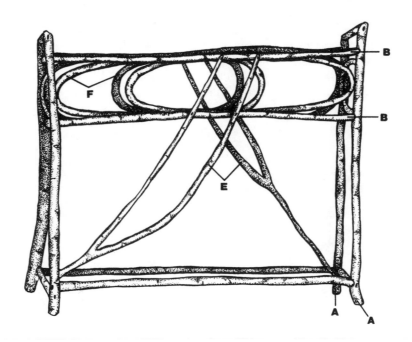

Adding the Willow Trim
1. Carefully bend and fit two arched willow branches F along the inside of the side legs and under the third side rails as shown in the diagram. Using thin finishing nails, nail in place.

2. Carefully bend a thin willow branch into an oval shape, positioning it between side rails one and two, as pictured. Using thin finishing nails, nail in place.

3. Carefully bend more thin willow shoots into a design and nail between beams B1 and B2 in both the front and the back, as pictured. This is a good time to let your imagination loose. Fill in as much or as little as you desire.

Finishing

This practical and well-proportioned plant stand can be finished in a variety of ways. Painting it white or dark green recalls nineteenth century fern stands, while shiny black adds a timeless quality. You may decide to paint each twig a different color, creating a unique effect for use indoors or out.

H ERB/F LOWER
D RYING R ACK

It probably takes longer to locate the triple forked willow twig than it does to construct this handy herb/flower drying rack. The lyrical shape of this piece combines the strength and beauty of willow, however, many other saplings or prunable branches such as alder or hazel may also be used. Make several of these to hang hats in the mudroom or kitchen towels in the pantry. Always be on the lookout for interesting forked twigs to help you create some original designs.

M ATERIALS

Use three-forked pliable twig 55" long with a base diameter of 2" tapering to 1", and a selection of twigs ⅛" to ¼" in diameter and 8" to 10" long. Galvanized flathead nails (#4p and #6p) and ¾" paneling finishing nails are also required.

T OOLS

- Single bit axe for felling trees or crosscut hand saw
- Clippers or garden shears
- Marking pencil

- Ruler or measuring tape
- Drill with a selection of bits
- Hammer
- Safety goggles
- Work gloves

HERB/FLOWER DRYING RACK CUTTING CHART

NAME OF PART	QUANTITY	DIAMETER (INCHES)	LENGTH (INCHES)	DESCRIPTION
Rack A	1	1–2	55	3-forked/pliable
Pegs	10	⅛–¼	8–10	straight or forked

DIRECTIONS

Cutting the Branches
1. Cut one 2" diameter 3-forked twig for rack A, 55" long.
2. Cut ten ⅛" to ¼" diameter twigs for the pegs B, each approximately 9" long.

Building the Rack
1. Carefully bend the ends of the forked branches together so that they gracefully fit together without pressure. Drill a pilot hole from the back through the ends of two twigs and partially through the front twig. Attach a galvanized nail from the back to join the three forked ends together.
2. Position the pegs B across the ledge of branches at points approximately 4" apart. Arrange the pegs so that some are resting over a branch, and others are situated under the branch.
3. Drill pilot holes at the points where the pegs meet the rack branches. Nail in place using the thin paneling nails.

Suggestions for Installing the Rack
1. Fasten eye-hooks to the top back twig and place cup-hooks on the wall.

2. Tie heavy twine from end-to-end of the rack, and hang it from a decorative picture hook.
3. Build a narrow wall shelf and rest the rack on top of the shelf, permitting the pegs to extend over the edge.

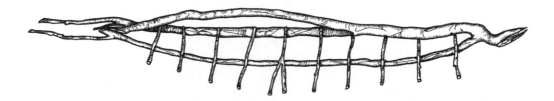

Finishing

This simple rack provides a charming place to display bundles of dried herbs and flowers. To enliven the spirit of a room, however, you may want to paint it. When choosing a color allow nature's palette to be your guide, such as the soft green of new-mown hay or the vibrant pink of a summer sunset.

D OLL C RADLE

Craft this charming 14" x 20" x 24"-high doll cradle for your favorite doll collector, or to add a nostalgic bit of country style to your own room. This old-
fashioned design, with its bonnet of tendrils and curlicues, can add just a touch of
enchantment.

MATERIALS

Use willow, alder, cedar, or any pliable branches. Lengths will range from 9" to 42"
long and from ½" to ¾" in diameter. You will also need a selection of vines, at least
13" long, in order to weave the bonnet. Two pieces of weathered box wood or ¼"
pine (3" x 16") are needed for the rockers. You'll also need galvanized box nails
(#2p and #4p), 1" finishing nails, string, and about 36" of heavy gauge wire.

T O O L S
- Single bit axe for felling trees
- Crosscut hand saw
- Clippers or garden shears
- Ruler or measuring tape
- Marking pencil
- Hammer
- Drill with a selection of bits
- Pliers
- Safety goggles
- Work gloves

D O L L   C R A D L E   C U T T I N G   C H A R T

NAME OF PART	QUANTITY	DIAMETER (INCHES)	LENGTH (INCHES)	DESCRIPTION
Footboard supports A	2	¾	10	hardwood/or pliable
Front brace B	1	½	9½	hardwood/or pliable
Front brace B	1	½	9½	forked
Footboard bar C	1	¾	14	hardwood/or pliable
Headboard frame D	1	½	40	pliable
Back braces E	3	½	11	hardwood/or pliable
Side rails F	6	¾	20	hardwood/or pliable
Bottom beams G	3	¾	20	hardwood/or pliable
Bonnet ribs H	3	½	41	pliable
Back bonnet supports I	3	¾	9–11	hardwood/or pliable
Vine	selection	–	13	with tendrils

D I R E C T I O N S

Cutting the Branches

1. Cut two ¾" diameter branches for footboard supports A, each 10" long.

2. Cut two (one forked) ½" diameter branches for front braces B, each 9½" long.
3. Cut one ¾" diameter branch for footboard bar C, 14" long.
4. Cut one ½" diameter branch for headboard frame D, 40" long.
5. Cut three ½" diameter branches for back braces E, each 11" long.
6. Cut six ¾" diameter branches for side rails F, each 20" long.
7. Cut three ¾" diameter branches for bottom beams G, each 20" long.
8. Cut three ½" diameter pliable branches for bonnet ribs H, each 41" long.
9. Cut three ¾" diameter branches for back bonnet supports I, each 9" to 11" long.
10. Using a pencil, draw a suitable curve at one end of the 3" x 16" rocker wood. Using the hand saw, cut along the edge of the curve, forming one rocker. Repeat with remaining 3" x 16" wood for the other rocker and lay them aside.
11. Cut pieces of vine in 12" to 14" lengths, remembering to keep the natural tendrils as much as possible.

Laying Out the Sub-Assembly

1. Butt lower front brace B between the two footboard supports A, 6" from the bottom of both A pieces. Join B to A by drilling through A and into the ends of B. Nail from the outside.
2. Overlap footboard bar C across the top of both footboard supports A. Drill pilot holes and nail in place from the top of footboard bar C.
3. Butt forked upper footboard brace B between both A supports, centering between lower footboard brace B and upper footboard bar C. Drill pilot holes and nail in place from the outside of both A supports.
4. Carefully bend headboard frame D into a U-shaped arch. Using the string, tie the ends together to keep the arch shape. There should be about a 10" space between the two ends.
5. Lay headboard frame D on a worktable. Six inches from the bottom of the arched headboard frame, butt the lower back brace E between the two ends of the headboard frame. Drill pilot holes and nail in place from the outside of the arch. Join top back brace E, butting it between the arch at a position 5" higher than the lower back brace. Drill and nail in place from the outside of the arch. Position middle back brace E between the first two back braces. Drill pilot holes and nail in place as before.

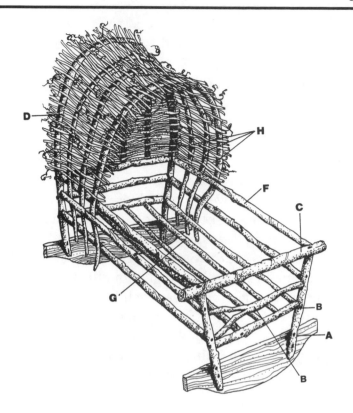

6. Butt the 11" back bonnet support I between the center of headboard frame D and top back brace E. Drill pilot holes and nail in place from the top of D and the bottom of E.

7. Repeat step 6 with the two 9" back bonnet supports, spacing them equally on either side of center branch I.

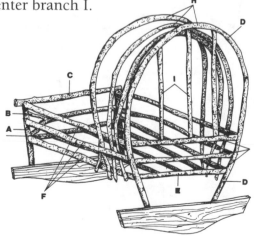

Joining the Sub-Assemblies

1. Butt lower side rail F between the footboard assembly and the headboard frame assembly where lower back brace E meets D and lower front brace B meets A. Drill pilot holes and nail in place from the front and back. Join two more side rails F at the middle and upper points of the same side. Join the three remaining side rails to the opposite side in the same fashion.

2. Add the first bonnet rib H, positioning it on lower side rail F 3" forward of headboard frame D. Weave the rib under middle side rail F and over top side rail F. Gently form the arched hoop shape to match the shape of the headboard frame. Finish the first rib by weaving the loose end over and under upper middle F rails on the other side of the cradle. If necessary, drill through both ends and nail to the bottom side rails.

3. Repeat steps 1 and 2 with the other two bonnet ribs. Adjust the ribs so that they slant forward. You should see a slight angle from the front back frame D.

4. Weave the heavy gauge wire under and over each bonnet rib H, leaving desired spacing between the ribs. This will help keep the ribs in place. Wrap one end of the wire around the front rib and the other end around headboard frame D. Using the pliers, fasten the wire to itself. The vine weaving will hide the wire, which may be removed after the piece has sufficiently dried.

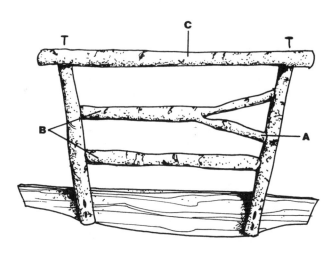

Adding the Rockers

1. Place one precut rocker inside footboard supports A. Drill pilot holes and nail in place using two to three nails for each side.

2. Place the other precut rocker inside headboard frame D. Drill and nail in place using two to three nails for each side.

Vine-Weaving the Bonnet
1. Weave the back first. Weave under and over back bonnet supports I, permitting the ends to extend past headboard frame D on both sides.
2. Weave under and over bonnet ribs H in the same manner, until bonnet supports I and ribs H are completely filled. Trim any uneven ends.

Finishing
The contrast of branches and vines is enhanced if this piece is left in its natural state. (Note: This cradle is not safe for infants.)

Five-sided Ottoman or Planter cube

This 24" square, 18" high cube is so handy that I cannot think of a room where it would not be useful. Any type of wood can be used to build the cube; you might consider using a variety in order to achieve a distinctive contrast. Once you have mastered the simple technique, try making these cubes in various sizes, or building a rectangle to fit at the foot of a bed. The cube's handcrafted beauty helps to blur the boundary between indoors and out. They are just as useful on the porch filled with geraniums as they are in the living room used as ottomans.

MATERIALS

Use such wood as willow, birch, beech, cedar, or hickory. You will need 50 straight twigs, 22" long and 1" in diameter. You will also require two straight wires, 60" long and ⅛" in diameter; one piece of board, at least 22" long, to make a jig; and one large nail to use with the jig.

172

TOOLS

- ◆ Axe or saw for cutting trees
- ◆ Crosscut hand saw
- ◆ Ruler
- ◆ Marking pencil
- ◆ Drill and a selection of bits
- ◆ Wire clippers

FIVE-SIDED OTTOMAN CUTTING CHART

NAME OF PART	QUANTITY	DIAMETER (INCHES)	LENGTH (INCHES)	DESCRIPTION
Twigs	50	1	22	straight
Board (for jig)	1		22	any width

DIRECTIONS

Cutting the Branches
    1. Cut 50 1" diameter branches, 22" long.

Making the Jig
    1. Drill two holes 18" apart in a straight board that is at least 22" long.

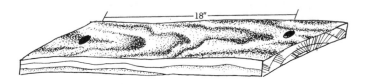

Drilling the Branches
    1. In 48 of the branches, drill holes 18" apart. Center them using the jig as your guide. (Note: To drill the second hole in each twig, place the nail in the first drilled hole through the jig into the branch. This holds the jig in place and ensures accuracy.) Make sure the diameter of the hole is large enough to allow you to thread the wire through the hole.

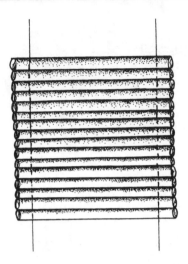

Assembling the Cube

1. String the drilled branches onto the two straight pieces of wire. Place the first branch in the middle of both wires. Continue stringing from both directions equally, until 18" of the wire is covered with 16 branches.

2. The bottom of the cube is now complete. Bend the bare wire upward to form two U-shaped wires. There should be about 15" of wire at each end of the threaded twigs.

3. Add two more drilled branches perpendicular to those already strung to form the foundation bottom. These will be on two opposite wires.

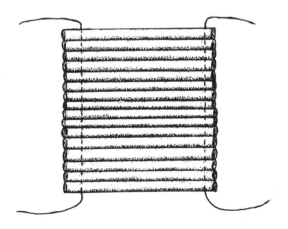

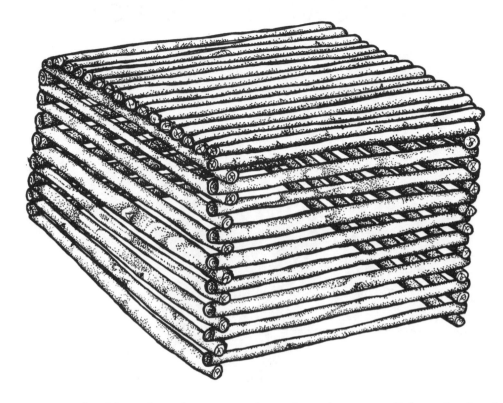

4. Continue building by alternating branches (one parallel with the base branches, one perpendicular, one parallel, etc.) until all but the last two branches have been added. Using wire clippers, cut the wires so that they will extend three-quarters of the way through the remaining top two branches.
5. Drill the last two branches using the jig, only one-quarter to one-third of the way through each end.
6. Tap the top two branches in place over the extended wire, being careful that you don't let the sharp wire ends come through.

Finishing

With the enormous variety of colors available, you are sure to find a way to enhance your cube if you choose to paint it. Remember one fanciful color can be a striking addition to any room. Individual taste will dictate the cushion fabric if you choose to use the cube as extra seating or as an ottoman.

Magazine Rack

Almost any room in the house will benefit from the addition of this well crafted, functional piece. Show off your ability to bend supple branches and, at the same time, create a handy holder to accommodate a bundle of assorted magazines.

MATERIALS

Any hardwood (such as birch, beech, or cherry) may be used. You will need lengths ranging from 6½" to 12", all 1" in diameter. You will also need five forked branches, 20" long, and three or four that are 12" long. Pliable branches (such as willow, alder, or cedar) in lengths from 24" to 50" and with diameters from ½" to 1" are also necessary. Use galvanized flathead nails in assorted sizes (#2p, #4p, #6p, and #8p).

T O O L S

- ♦ Single bit axe for felling trees
- ♦ Crosscut hand saw
- ♦ Clippers or garden shears
- ♦ Ruler or measuring tape
- ♦ Marking pencil
- ♦ Drill with a selection of bits
- ♦ Hammer
- ♦ Safety goggles
- ♦ Work gloves

M A G A Z I N E   R A C K   C U T T I N G   C H A R T

NAME OF PART	QUANTITY	DIAMETER (INCHES)	LENGTH (INCHES)	DESCRIPTION
Lower side of rails A	2	1	6½	hardwood
Lower front rails/ bottom supports B	2	1	20	forked, hardwood
Frame bow C	2	¾	50	pliable
Frame bow C1	2	½	41	pliable
Frame bow C2	2	½	36	pliable
Frame bow C3	2	½	31	pliable
Frame bow C4	2	¼	24	pliable
Frame bow C5	2	¼	20	pliable
Side supports D	3–4	1	12	forked, hardwood
Handle H	1	¾	50	pliable

D I R E C T I O N S

Cutting the Branches
1. Cut two 1" diameter branches for lower side rails A, each 6½" long.
2. Cut two 1" diameter forked branches for lower front rails/bottom supports B, each 20" long.

3. Cut two ¾" diameter pliable branches for frame bow C, each 50" long.
4. Cut two ½" diameter pliable branches for frame bow C1, each 41" long.
5. Cut two ½" diameter pliable branches for frame bow C2, each 36" long.
6. Cut two ½" diameter pliable branches for frame bow C3, each 31" long.
7. Cut two ¼" diameter pliable branches for frame bow C4, each 24" long.
8. Cut two ¼" diameter pliable branches for frame bow C5, each 20" long.
9. Cut three or four 1" diameter forked branches for side supports D, each 12" long. (Note: The number of forked branches you will require is determined by the placement of the fork in branch D.)
10. Cut one ¾" diameter pliable branch for handle H, 50" long.

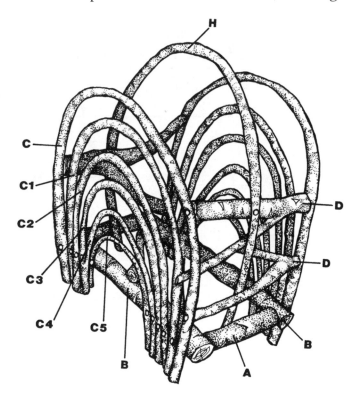

Laying Out the Sub-Assembly
1. Lay out lower side rails A and front rails/bottom supports B on a worktable. Assemble a rectangle by butting the two lower side rails A against the two forked lower front rail/bottom supports B. Be sure to arrange the forked branches so that they will form a suitable bottom for the rack. This is achieved by overlapping the forks that extend from the main branch.

2. Drill and nail in place with pilot hole and nail construction. Nail from the outside of B through to A, using a #6p or #8p nail.

3. Drill pilot holes and nail the overlapping, forked branch parts of B to the opposite side B, thus forming the bottom.

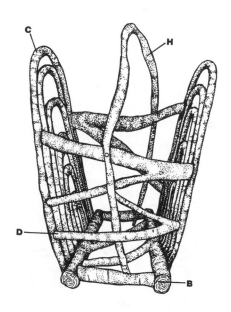

Attaching the Sides (Frame Bows)

1. The center point of the first bow should be approximately 16" high from branch B. The frame bows C to C5 form the legs. Allow 3" to extend below branch B when joining the bows to B. Drill pilot holes and nail one end of B from the outside, allowing 3" to extend beyond lower front rail/bottom support B. Gently bend the branch to form an arch. Bring the free end down to the opposite end of the same branch B, remembering to allow 3" to extend beyond B. Drill pilot holes and nail C to B from the outside.

2. Continue to add frame bows C1 to C5, in consecutive order, following the procedure in step 1.

3. Repeat on the opposite side.

Connecting the Bows and Adding the Handle

1. Stand your rack on the worktable. Arrange forked side supports D between outside frame bows C. Depending on the size of branch used, you will want to add one or two D branches to each side between the front and back frame

bows. When you are satisfied with the placement, drill and nail forked side supports D to frame bows C from the outside of C.

2. To attach handle H, gently bend it into a U-shaped arch, carefully placing each side between forked side supports D and on the inside of lower siderails A. Drill pilot holes and nail in place at the points where H meets A and D on both sides.

Finishing

The rustic texture of the bark and subtle coloring of the arched branches is often best left natural. However, for greater contrast, you may decide to paint your magazine rack. Remember, a flourish of vivid color is always more exciting than a drab color. Try red for impact or a mustard yellow that is reminiscent of early milk paint.

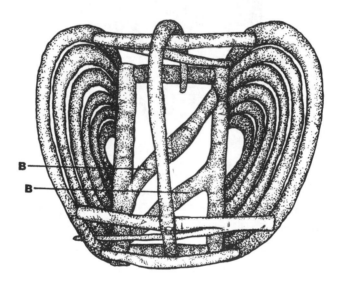

PLATE STAND

This four-foot stand is a perfect example of thinking in terms of "twig." Its prototype was a nineteenth century French plate stand discovered at a country auction. The plate stand's graceful, simple shape is perfect for storing and displaying a multitude of items in any room. The key to its construction is careful tapering at the ends of the shelf support branches to form secure "shelves."

MATERIALS

Be sure you choose straight but pliable branches of willow, alder, cedar, or another similar wood. Lengths will range from 7" to 48", and diameters from ¼" to 1". You'll need pliable (green) branches for the slight bending that will be needed to create a straight stand. You will also need #2p galvanized box nails. (Box nails are flathead nails, lighter in weight than common galvanized flathead nails.)

TOOLS

- Single bit axe for felling trees
- Crosscut hand saw
- Clippers or garden shears
- Ruler or measuring tape
- Marking pencil
- ⅜" variable-speed drill
- Hammer
- Sharp pocket knife for tapering the ends
- Safety goggles
- Work gloves

PLATE STAND CUTTING CHART

NAME OF PART	QUANTITY	DIAMETER (INCHES)	LENGTH (INCHES)	DESCRIPTION
Legs A	3	¾–1	48	forked at one end straight, pliable
Shelf supports B	3	¾	12	straight, pliable
Shelf supports B1	3	¾	11	straight, pliable
Shelf supports B2	3	½	10	straight, pliable
Shelf supports B3	3	½	9	straight, pliable
Shelf supports B4	3	½	8	straight, pliable
Shelf supports B5	3	½	7	straight, pliable

DIRECTIONS

Cutting the Branches
1. Cut three straight ¾" to 1" diameter branches for legs A, each 48" long. Try to find branches that have a natural crook or fork at approximately the same place on one end, as pictured.
2. Cut three straight ¾" diameter branches for shelf supports B, each 12" long.
3. Cut three straight ¾" diameter branches for shelf supports B1, each 11" long.

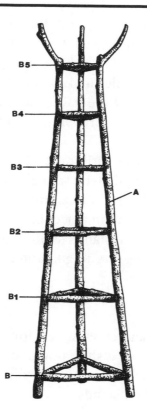

4. Cut three straight ½" diameter branches for shelf supports B2, each 10" long.
5. Cut three straight ½" diameter branches for shelf supports B3, each 9" long.
6. Cut three straight ½" diameter branches for shelf supports B4, each 8" long.
7. Cut three straight ½" diameter branches for shelf supports B5, each 7" long.

Building the Stand
1. Hold legs A upright and choose an inside edge of each branch.
2. Place the three legs A on a worktable. On the inside of each leg A, make a pencil mark 2½" up from the bottom of each leg.
3. Make another pencil mark 10" above the first marks. Continue to mark the branches in the following manner: make two more marks, each 9" above the one before. Then make two more marks, each 8" above the last two. This will give you six marks in all.
4. Beginning with the lowest shelf supports B, use a sharp pocket knife (or garden shears) to taper the ends of B to approximately one-third of the branch diameter (see diagram). Butt B against leg A at the first pencil mark and check

for a tight fit. Taper the remaining ends of B. Butt each B to the leg A against which that piece will be nailed, and check for a tight fit.

5. Drill pilot holes through the ends of B into the two legs A at the pencil marks. Join B to A, lining up the pilot holes and nailing only three-quarters of the way through. Leave one-quarter of the nail exposed until the stand is completely assembled. This prevents the driven nails from being loosened as you proceed.

6. Repeat from step 4, tapering, fitting, drilling, and nailing the remaining two B branches to legs A, forming an equilateral triangle. Two nails will be placed at each B junction along the leg A. Proceed carefully when drilling and nailing.

7. Continue to taper, fit, drill, and nail in place the remaining shelf supports B1 through B5. Make sure your piece stands straight and even as you proceed. Bend and adjust the legs as necessary to guarantee balanced "shelves" and a straight plate stand.

Finishing

The natural beauty of wood is a perfect showcase for a wide variety of kitchen items, such as pots and pans, casserole dishes, bowls, or table linen. For an exciting accent, paint two of your completed structures brilliant yellow and place them in a formal living room to use as plant stands.

Miniature Chairs

These whimsical chairs were originally designed for a national publication when its crafts editor needed tree decorations for a woodland Christmas story. Enlisting the help of family members, we built 20 of these 10-inch-high chairs. Hanging on the fresh evergreen boughs, their playful shapes helped to create a festive mood. Regardless of the season, however, you can combine these natural ingredients to build your own collectables to enjoy anytime, or to give as a gift for birthdays, baby showers, or house warmings. Miniature chairs are also a perfect project for people with limited work space.

MATERIALS

You will need to use pliable branches such as willow, alder, or cedar. Lengths will range from 4" to 22", and branches should be to ⅛" to ¼" in diameter. Wood scraps (⅛" to ¼" thick and 3¾" by 3¾" wide) are required for the seats (wood shingles work nicely). You will also need 1" oak-colored, interior panel finishing nails and rubber bands or string.

TOOLS

- Clippers or garden shears
- Tack hammer
- Coping saw
- Safety goggles
- Ruler or measuring tape
- Work gloves
- Marking pencil

MINIATURE CHAIRS CUTTING CHART
LADDER-BACK CHAIR

NAME OF PART	QUANTITY	DIAMETER (INCHES)	LENGTH (INCHES)	DESCRIPTION
Back legs A	2	⅛–¼	10–11	pliable
Front legs/arms B	2	⅛–¼	10–11	pliable
Bottom braces C	4	⅛–¼	4	pliable
Ladder-backs D	3	⅛–¼	4	pliable
Top rail E	1	⅛–¼	6	pliable

WRAP-AROUND ARMCHAIR

NAME OF PART	QUANTITY	DIAMETER (INCHES)	LENGTH (INCHES)	DESCRIPTION
Back legs A	2	⅛–¼	10	pliable
Front leg/ arm wrap B	2	⅛–¼	20–22	pliable
Bottom braces C	4	⅛–¼	4	pliable
Top arched rail D	1	⅛–¼	22	pliable

LADDER-BACK CHAIR
DIRECTIONS

Cutting the Branches
  1. Cut two branches for back legs A, each 10" to 11" long.

2. Cut two branches for front legs/arms B, each 10" to 11" long.
3. Cut four branches for bottom braces C, each 4" long.
4. Cut three branches for ladder-backs D, each 4" long.
5. Cut one branch for top rail E, 6" long.

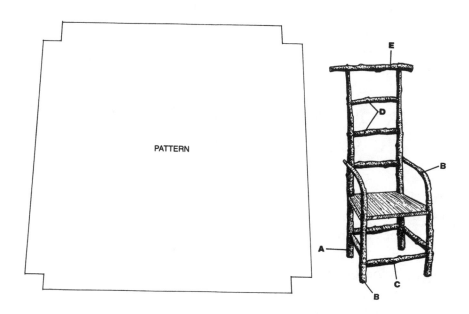

Making the Ladder-Back Chair

1. Using tracing paper, trace the pattern provided. Transfer the shape onto the wood scraps and cut the seat with corners to size, using the coping saw.
2. Position the two back legs A in the seat back at the two corner cutouts. Three inches of the leg should extend below the seat corner. Using the finishing nails, nail the two back legs A to the seat back at both corner cutout locations.
3. Position the two front legs/arms B in the seat front at the two corner cutouts (again, with 3" of the leg extending below the seat corner). Using the finishing nails, nail the two front legs B to the seat front at both corner cutout locations. Allow the extended arms to remain unattached until the braces are added.
4. Butt lower braces C between the front and back legs, about 1" from the bottom of each leg. Nail in place through the sides of the legs.

5. Carefully bend the arms toward back legs A, and nail in place where the ends of B meet A.
6. Arrange ladder-backs D approximately 1½" apart above the seat and between the two back legs A. Join D parts to the two back legs A, nailing from the sides of the legs.
7. Overlap top rail E across the two extending back legs A. Nail in place from the top of E into the two A parts.
8. Wrap rubber bands or tie string around the bottom of the legs. This keeps the chair straight until it dries thoroughly (usually in five to 10 days).

WRAP-AROUND ARMCHAIR
DIRECTIONS

Cutting the Branches
1. Cut two branches for back legs A, each 10" long.
2. Cut two branches for front leg/arm wrap B, each 20" to 22" long.
3. Cut four branches for bottom braces C, each 4" long.
4. Cut one branch for top arched rail D, 22" long.

Making the Wrap-Around Armchair
1. Using tracing paper, trace the pattern provided. Transfer onto the wood scraps and cut the seat with corners to size, using the coping saw.
2. Position the back legs A in the seat back at the two corner cutouts. Three inches of the leg should extend below the seat corner. Using the finishing nails, nail the two back legs A to the seat back at both corner cutout locations.
3. Position the front leg/arm wraps B in the seat front at the two corner cutouts (again, with 3" of the leg extending below the seat corner). Using the finishing nails, nail the two front legs B to the seat front at both corner cutout locations. Leave the extended arms unattached until the braces are added.
4. Butt braces C between the front and back legs, about ½" from the bottom of each leg. Nail in place through the outside of the legs.
5. Carefully bend each extended leg/arm wrap B toward the corresponding back leg. The extension should rest against the outside, forming a hoop. Then bring it around and forward on the outside of the opposite back leg. Nail it to the seat at the point where they meet. Tuck the ends inside the bottom braces.

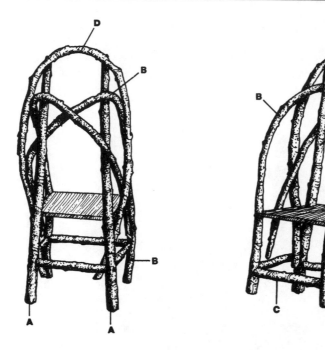

6. Center and overlap the top arched rail D against the top of back legs A. Nail in place from the top of D into the two legs A. Carefully bend both top rails D to form a hoop. Tuck the ends inside the bottom braces, and nail the sides of top rail D to the seat.

7. Wrap rubber bands or string around the bottom of legs A. This keeps the chair straight until it dries thoroughly (usually in five to 10 days).

Finishing

For an imaginative centerpiece, nestle several miniature chairs among pots of trailing ivy, or paint a group of them in a variety of colors and line them up on your mantel. These chairs can add imagination and flair to even the most sophisticated of rooms.

CANDLESTICKS

These easy-to-make candlesticks with a woodland touch will brighten any room. Cluster them for a mantel decoration, or arrange them into a tabletop centerpiece. A pair of these, bundled like little logs and tied with twine, make a welcome gift any time of the year. Cut the twin twig candlestick from an appropriate log; the single candleholders from white birch logs of assorted heights.

MATERIALS

Choose a hardwood such as white birch, beech, maple or cherry. The twin candlestick requires a double branch of white birch, 9" long x 3" in diameter for each branch. Individual candleholders vary in height from 4" to 9". Consider using foil mini-muffin liners or scrap foil to prevent wax spills on the logs. To measure the openings, keep candles nearby.

TOOLS

- ♦ Crosscut hand saw
- ♦ Ruler or measuring tape
- ♦ Marking pencil
- ♦ Electric drill with bit the diameter of candle (Note: This is usually a ¾" bit)
- ♦ Safety goggles
- ♦ Work gloves

DIRECTIONS

Even out bottom of logs with the saw so they stand firmly upright. Measure and mark the center top of each log. Using the correct size bit, drill a hole 1" deep at the center mark of each log. Center the candle in a mini-muffin liner and push it into the hole. (Never leave these candles burning unattended.)

Finishing
Subtle hues and natural markings characterize these candleholders. As it would be difficult improve upon them, they are best left in their natural state.

CHAPTER 6

Garden Accessories

GARDEN TRELLIS

Rustic trellises add charm to any garden and are surprisingly easy to construct. The version shown here is just one example of what can be done with some white birch poles and a forked, flexible willow shoot. Be on the lookout for interesting center loops and swags in saplings of alder, hazel, maple, locust or sycamore. This trellis, made for morning-glories, would work just as nicely for any green or flowering vine.

MATERIALS

Use woods like birch, beech, cedar, maple or willow. Lengths range from 22" to 82" with diameters from ¾" to 1". Locate a forked willow, or similar pliable wood, ¼" to ½" in diameter and 35" to 45" in length for the center trim. Galvanized flat-head nails in assorted sizes (#4p, #6p, and #8p) and finishing nails (¾" and 1") will also be required.

TOOLS

- Single bit axe for felling trees
- Crosscut hand saw
- Clippers or garden shears
- Ruler or measuring tape
- Work gloves
- Drill with a selection of bits
- Hammer
- Safety goggles
- Work gloves
- Pocket knife (optional)

GARDEN TRELLIS CUTTING CHART

NAME OF PART	QUANTITY	DIAMETER (INCHES)	LENGTH (INCHES)	DESCRIPTION
Side supports A	2	1½	82	straight
Overlap beams B	2	1	13	straight
Cross braces C	4	¾–1	30	straight/forked
Center loop D	1	¼–½	35–45	forked/pliable

DIRECTIONS

Cutting the Branches
1. Cut two 1½ diameter branches for side supports A, each 82" long.
2. Cut two 1" diameter branches for the overlap beams B, each 13" long.
3. Cut four ¾" to 1" diameter branches for the cross braces C, each 30" long.

4. Cut one ¼" to ½" diameter pliable forked twig for the center loop D, 35" to 45" long.

Laying Out the Sub-Assembly
1. Using a pencil and ruler, mark the points where the overlap beams B will be added to the side supports A to form the basic framework for the trellis. Place the top beam 9" from the top of each leg. The bottom beam is placed 12" up from the bottom of each leg. Each beam extends approximately 6" beyond the side supports.
2. Drill pilot holes through the overlap beams and the side supports from the back of trellis. Nail in place using galvanized nails.

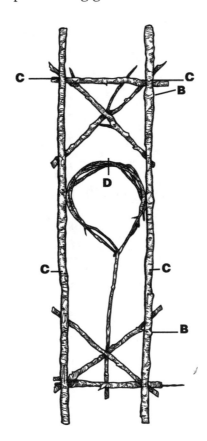

Adding the Cross Braces
1. From the back of the overlap beam B, place cross brace C at a pleasing angle and nail in place using pilot hole and nail construction.

2 Repeat with remaining cross braces at the top and the bottom of the construction.

Adding the Willow Trim
1. Carefully bend the forked willow into a loop, wrapping and twisting the two pliable ends over each other in a wreath shape. Center the loop and nail in place to the inside edges of the side supports using finishing nails.
2. Nail the willow handle in place in the same manner.

Finishing
A twig trellis usually lasts for two to four years outdoors without any protective coating. Making a trellis like this is easy to make and you won't mind replacing it after a few years. Also try using cedar poles, grapevine and Virginia creeper.

WATTLE-WEAVE TRELLIS

Trellises add a strong sense of form and function in a garden, providing the perfect support for a variety of vines and climbing flowers. This willow fan-tail trellis, measuring 80" x 36", takes the basic trellis shape a step further and adds the centuries-old technique of wattle weaving to create a dramatic outdoor sculpture. The wattle-weave trellis is particularly well-suited for masses of climbing roses or clematis.

MATERIALS

Use any pliable twigs such as willow, alder, hazel or poplar; the sturdiest ones for the uprights and the more flexible for weaving. Supple vines, such as grapevine or virginia creeper, are good weaving materials as well. You will need five lengths 80" long, and ¾" to ⅞" in diameter.

You will also need a bottom brace, 16" long and at least ¾" in diameter; and a top brace 55" long and at least ¾" in diameter. Collect approximately 25 twigs from ¼" to ¾" in diameter and 16" to 55" long for weaving. Ten galvanized nails are required.

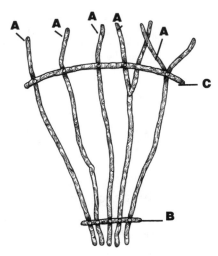

TOOLS

- ◆ Single bit axe for felling trees
- ◆ Crosscut hand saw
- ◆ Clippers or garden shears
- ◆ Ruler or measuring tape
- ◆ Marking pencil
- ◆ Drill with a selection of bits
- ◆ Hammer
- ◆ Safety goggles
- ◆ Work gloves

WATTLE-WEAVE TRELLIS CUTTING CHART

NAME OF PART	QUANTITY	DIAMETER (INCHES)	LENGTH (INCHES)	DESCRIPTION
Vertical supports A	5	¾–1	80	pliable
Bottom brace B	1	¾–1	16	straight

NAME OF PART	QUANTITY	DIAMETER (INCHES)	LENGTH (INCHES)	DESCRIPTION
Top brace C	1	¾–1	55	straight
Bottom weavers	10	¼	16	pliable
Middle weavers	8	¼–½	40	pliable
Top weavers	5	½–1	55	pliable

DIRECTIONS

Cutting the Branches

1. Cut five ¾" to ⅞" diameter branches for vertical supports A, each 80" long. Note: Try to include some forked branches as shown in illustration.
2. Cut one ¾" to 1" diameter straight branch for the bottom brace B, 16" long.
3. Cut one ¾" to 1" diameter branch for the top brace C, 55" long.
4. Cut ¼" to 1" diameter weavers; ten bottom twigs, 16" long; eight middle twigs, 40" long; and five top twigs, 55" long.

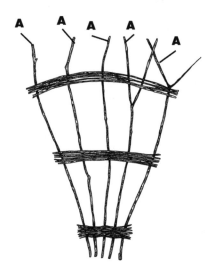

Assembling the Trellis

1. Place the five vertical supports A on a work surface and arrange them so that they are spaced 4" apart at the bottom and 10" to 14" apart at the top.

2. Overlap the bottom horizontal brace B across the five vertical supports A, 10" from the bottom. Drill and nail in place.

3. Overlap the top brace C across the vertical supports, at approximately 14" to 16" from the top. Drill and nail in place.

Adding the Wattle Weaving

Begin the weaving adjacent to the installed bottom brace B. Interlace the slender pliable twigs or vines over and under the vertical supports A. Continue in the same fashion, at the top adjacent to the top brace C. Repeat the weaving with the middle weavers approximately 36" up from the bottom.

Finishing

Coating the exposed ends with a non-toxic commercial sealer may extend the life of the trellis, but it is not necessary. Left in its natural state, it will weather gracefully and blend into its surroundings.

BASIC BIRD FEEDER

Bird feeders come in a surprising array of shapes and sizes. Nature enthusiasts and more importantly, birds seem especially fond of this model. Easy enough to make in a day, you may want several to hang around your property or to give as gifts. Be sure to search the firewood pile for nicely marked logs and branches. Suspended from a tree limb or mounted on a post this feeder blends gracefully with nature.

MATERIALS

Choose two 6" diameter white birch slices, 1" thick for the top, and 2" thick for the bottom. Note: Any hardwood such as hickory, maple or beech may be used. You will also need one 1½" diameter branch, 6" long for the center post. Four 1½" galvanized roofing nails and a screw eye for hanging are also neccessary.

TOOLS

- ♦ Single bit axe for felling trees, if you don't have a wood pile
- ♦ Crosscut hand saw
- ♦ Sandpaper (optional)
- ♦ Ruler or measuring tape
- ♦ Marking pencil
- ♦ Woodcarver's gouge and mallet
- ♦ Drill and a selection of bits
- ♦ Hammer
- ♦ Clippers or garden shears
- ♦ Safety goggles
- ♦ Heavy duty work gloves

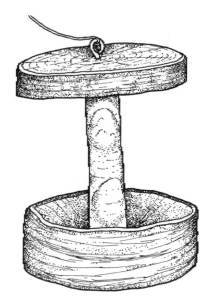

DIRECTIONS

Begin by sanding on both sides of the top wood slice and only one side of the bottom slice.

Shaping the Feeder
Caution: The gouge is a potentially dangerous hand tool. Wear heavy duty work gloves and safety glasses to avoid cuts and flying wood chips.

1. With a dark pencil, mark a ½" margin around the circumference of the bottom wood slice.
2. Use the woodcarver's gouge and mallet to begin chipping a depression across the middle. Turn the wood slice as you work and continue to chip at an angle from opposite sides. Aim for a shallow angle along the rim with a concave bottom.
3. When the bottom has reached a depth of 1½", add the 6" long center post.

Assembling the Feeder
1. Center the 6" long post on the underside of the 1" thick top slice. Using pilot hole and nail construction with two nails, join the top piece to the post from the outside.
2. Position the 6" long center post in the base of the gouged out bottom. Attach the two pieces from the bottom, using two nails and pilot hole construction to avoid splitting the wood. Center and join the 1" thick remaining slice to the center post from the top.
3. Add a galvanized metal screw eye and rope for hanging, or mount on a post.

White Birch Bird House

Bird houses are not simply outdoor shelters these days; many now add a light-hearted sculptural charm indoors as well. This basic log birdhouse serves both purposes. The forked twig support is a simple tree hanger outdoors, an attached display easel indoors. A piece of a discarded pot found in the woods makes up the tin roof along with some fallen white birch limbs. The 1" diameter entrance is ideal for chickadees. To attract the nuthatch make the opening slightly larger, for the wren, the opening should be ⅞".

MATERIALS

Use a white birch log, 7" long and 5" in diameter, or other hardwoods such as beech, cherry, hickory or cedar. Locate a three-forked branch, 21" long and 1" in diameter for the whimsical hanger/easel. Try to find interesting material for the roof, such as tin cans, straw, clay tiles or roofing shingles. Galvanized flathead nails in assorted sizes, 1½" metal roofing nails, and 1" finishing nails are required to complete your project.

T O O L S

- ◆ Single bit axe for felling trees
- ◆ Coping saw
- ◆ Crosscut hand saw
- ◆ Ruler
- ◆ Marking pencil
- ◆ Carpenter's gouge or woodcarving chisel
- ◆ Mallet
- ◆ Brace and bit (optional)
- ◆ Drill with a selection of bits, including a woodboring bit
- ◆ Safety goggles
- ◆ Work gloves

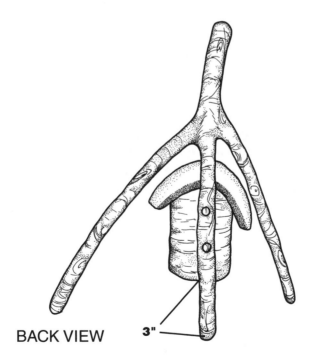

BACK VIEW   3"

DIRECTIONS

Note: The log requires a 3½" cavity for the nesting compartment. With luck, you will find a hollow, or partially hollow log created by time and nature. Most likely, however, you will have to bore out the center of the log yourself. One method is to use a power drill and make several large holes in a circular pattern, then further shape the opening with the chisel and mallet. A brace and bit work just as well but take longer. Choose a steel-shanked ratchet brace with a 10" sweep, and an expansive bit that makes a hole 3" across. This method may still require a chisel and mallet to make the cavity slightly larger.

1. Stand the 5" diameter, 7" long log on the work table. Draw a 3½" diameter circle on the bottom of the log.
2. Using one of the methods mentioned above, bore a 3½" diameter hole completely through the log.
3. Center a pencil mark 2½" down from the top of the log. Using the drill and woodboring bit, create a 1" opening through the log for the entrance hole.
4. Cut a ¼" thick piece of scrap wood the size of the bottom opening for the bird house floor. Fit the floor back in place and nail at an angle through the floor and the inside walls of the hollow log.

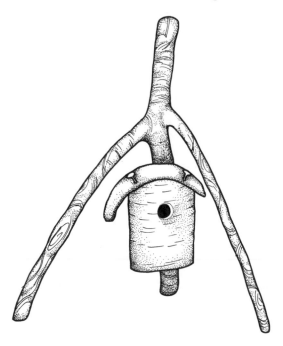

Completing the House

1. Cut and arrange roofing material of choice over the top, making sure the roof completely covers the opening to prevent rain from wetting the nesting area. Attach the tin roof with roofing nails.
2. To add the perch, attach a 1" high, 3" long scrap of white birch under the entrance with two finishing nails.
3. Butt the center branch of the three-forked twig firmly against the back of the house, allowing approximately 3" to extend below it. Using pilot hole and nail construction, attach the center branch to the back of the house. Trim the ends of the two remaining forks, making sure the forked twig easel stands straight.

CHAPTER 7

Bark and
Vine Projects

Although each type of natural material has its own unique uses, to my way of thinking, nothing is as versatile as tree bark. Throughout history, bark has been put to use in a variety of ways. Birch bark is the most commonly used, as its natural waxes make it waterproof. It is also very durable and remains in the soil after the tree's inner wood has rotted away. Many cultures have developed uses for bark. Native Americans used the tough bark of the white paper birch to cover the twig frames of their wigwams, and fastened large sheets of it over wooden frames to make canoes. They also made birch bark containers and, throughout the late 1800s and into the twentieth century, created birch bark souvenirs for the tourist trade. The Laplanders use bark to make plates and circular boxes, as well as for roofing shingles. In Switzerland, a large musical instrument called an alphorn, up to 15 feet long, is made out of birch bark.

My first bark basket was an antique one that I bought in Northern Canada about 20 years ago. The vendor told me it was made by a Cree Indian in the 1800s. Its sturdy shape fascinated me, and I still marvel at its simple charm. The bark of the birch is reversed, so that the paper white is on the inside and the reddish hue of the inner bark is displayed on the outside. The bottom and the side closing are laced together with a willow, and it has a bent willow handle. This basket has delighted me throughout the years, and has served to hold fresh or dried flowers (with a glass jar inside), French bread at a buffet dinner, and a heap of pine cones and red ribbons during the holidays.

My second experience with bark took place in North Carolina, where I discovered an Appalachian berry basket. This unique basket is folded from one piece of bark, and its cylindrical shape and the concave eye-shaped base are its distinctive features. I have seen similar baskets made by the Cherokee, and assume that the early mountaineers learned how to make this basket from them.

By the late 1800s, the Adirondack mountain region of northern New York State had become a fashionable resort area for wealthy industrialists like the Vanderbilts, the Whitneys, and the Rockefellers. Soon they were buying up vast acreage and lakefront property and hiring architects to design and build luxurious versions of rustic summer cabins. These summer play houses of the rich and famous became known as "the Great Camps," in contrast to the smaller camps that consisted of anything from a shanty to a group of canvas tents mounted on wooden platforms. Although the Great Camps were designed by their owners to yield a rustic and simple life, they were well-staffed by household help, gardeners and caretakers to provide all the comforts of the home. Many caretakers at the Great Camps spent much of the winter building rustic twig furniture for the camp owners and patiently overlaying the surfaces of cabinets, dressers and tables with sheets of bark. At the Great Camps an attempt was made to integrate natural elements from the outdoors into the inside living area. Today, their influence can be found across the country, from lodges at Yellowstone to the President's retreat at Camp David.

WORKING WITH BIRCH BARK

Bark taken from freshly cut trees is usually pliable enough to use within a day or two. If, however, you have to wait several days before you begin your project, it is a good idea to soak the bark in water. A walk through the woods will often lead you to pieces of naturally peeled bark that you can use for some of the projects.

BARK WOODS

Paper white birch, black birch, chestnut, box elder, eucalyptus, hickory, palm, tulip poplar (yellow poplar), white walnut, yew, mountain magnolia, ash, linden, and bass are all good barks to use for projects. Alder and fir might also be usable. It is a good idea to experiment with bark from local trees to see which are usable for projects.

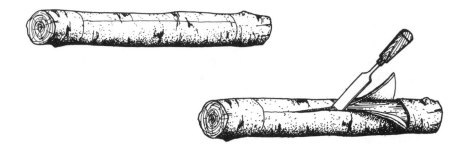

PEELING THE BARK

Use only bark from recently fallen trees. Do not peel bark from living trees. Stripping the bark from live trees will cause the tree to die.

To peel the bark from the branch, score a deep line lengthwise through the bark with a sharp knife. Make two cuts around the branch, marking the section of the bark to be removed. Place the top of a chisel along the scored line and gently tap it with a mallet. Continue until the section of bark is removed. If the project requires pressed bark, press the bark between heavy books or large flat rocks or bricks until ready to use. Depending on where you are comfortable working, pressing the bark can be done indoors or outdoors (see illustration). Although I have successfully peeled bark during all seasons, it is easiest in the summer when the sap is up.

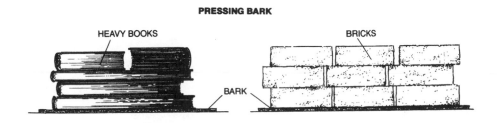

PRESSING BARK

HEAVY BOOKS

BRICKS

BARK

VINES

Those pesky bramble vines that often infest suburban yards and smother trees and bushes in the wild are another fine source of material. There is an almost limitless supply of free basketmaking materials growing along roadsides. In addition, pruning some of these vines enhances the surrounding countryside.

In recent years, grapevines have been widely used to make wonderful, decorative wreaths. I have found that the natural shape of the grapevine, with its whimsical tendrils, will work beautifully to create serviceable baskets and practical lampshades.

For those who have always wanted to weave baskets but who are intimidated by instructions that include splints and spokes, I have developed a very easy basketmaking technique.

GOOD VINES FOR PROJECTS

Bittersweet, Boston Ivy, clematis, grapevine, honeysuckle, ivy kudzu, Virginia creeper, and wisteria (ivy and grape) are vines that are easy to use. Blackberry and raspberry are useful too, but must be dehorned.

Bark Basket
with Handle

Perhaps because of its usefulness, this unadorned basket is one of the finest examples of bark work. This design, adapted from an original Native American container, transforms bark to basket in a remarkably simple way. Its classic shape, rooted deep in the history of basketmaking, continues to inspire new generations of craftspeople. The following directions are for a basket that is 10 inches high and seven inches in diameter.

MATERIALS

One sheet of peeled bark for the basket, 10" wide and 22" long, and one sheet of peeled bark for the bottom B, approximately 8" x 8", are required. You will also need two pliable branches for top and bottom rims C, approximately 30" long and ¼" to ½" in diameter; one pliable branch for handle D, 3½" long and ¾" in diameter; and peeled bark strips for lacing, ⅛" wide.

TOOLS

- Clippers or garden shears
- Ruler or measuring tape
- Marking pencil
- Scissors
- Leather hole punch or awl
- Large-eye needle and heavy thread (optional)

DIRECTIONS

Assembling the Basket

1. Using the hole punch (or awl) punch holes evenly approximately ¾" to 1" apart along all four sides of peeled bark piece A.

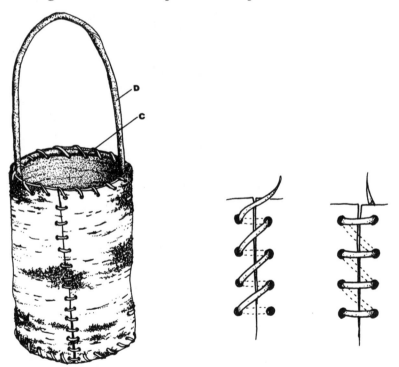

2. Lace the narrowest open ends of bark A together to form a circular shape, shown below. For increased strength, you may choose to lace all parts together with the needle and heavy thread first, and then add the peeled bark for embellishment.

Assembling the Bottom

1. Measuring the upper basket diameter for size, cut the 8" x 8" bark sheet into a 6½" to 7" diameter circle for bottom B. Punch holes ¾" to 1" apart along the outside edge.
2. Carefully bend bottom branch C into a ring and fit inside the bottom edge of A.
3. Fit bottom B inside the basket, resting against branch C. Pull lacing through the holes on the bottom of A, around C, and through the holes in B, as shown below.
4. Carefully bend top branch C into a ring and fit inside the top rim of A. Lace in place.

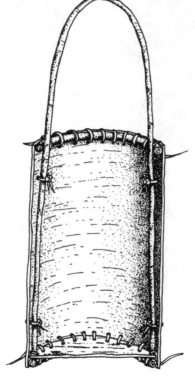

Adding the Handle

1. Gently bend branch D into a curved handle shape. Place ends inside the basket, resting them on the bottom. Punch small holes from the outside of A on either side of the handle near the top and bottom. Lace through the holes with strips of peeled bark, knotted and tied from the inside, as shown in drawing #3.

Bark Basket with Two Handles

You'll appreciate this handsome basket, usefulness aside, for its beautiful bark markings. Once you master the technique, you can easily adjust the size of your basket. The following directions are for a basket that is seven inches high, with an oval base that measures 7" x 18". This example requires four sheets of bark that are 12½" wide, and two sheets 14" wide.

MATERIALS

You will need one oval wood base, 7" x 18" and ½" thick. A selection of bark sheets, two 7" wide and 12" long for center parts A, and two 7" wide and 14" long for end parts B, will also be required. You will also need a selection of willow shoots or other pliable branches 36" to 48" long and ⅛" to ¼" in diameter for inside rim C; two ¾" wide pliable bark strips to form handles D, each 36" long; and one pliable branch to wrap the circumference E, 8' to 10' long and ⅛ to ½" in diameter. You will also need bark or vine strips for lacing, ¾" carpet tacks, contact cement, and heavy books or bricks for pressing the bark flat.

TOOLS

- ♦ Clippers or garden shears
- ♦ Ruler or measuring tape
- ♦ Marking pencil
- ♦ Scissors and sharp pocket knife
- ♦ Leather hole punch or awl
- ♦ Tack hammer
- ♦ Large-eye needle and heavy thread (optional)
- ♦ Spring-type clothespins

DIRECTIONS

Cutting the Bark Sheets

1. Place the flattened bark pieces on the worktable. Using the scissors and cutting with the grain, cut two pieces 7" wide and 12" long for center parts A.
2. Cut two pieces of bark 7" wide and 14" long for end parts B.

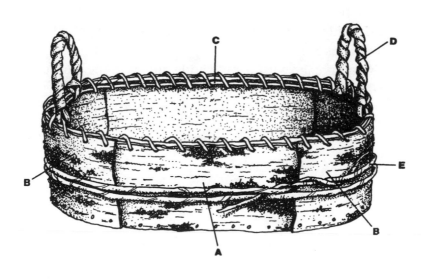

Building the Basket

1. Center one bark sheet A lengthwise along the outside rim of the 7" x 18" oval wooden base. Using the carpet tacks, fasten the bark to the base at evenly spaced intervals.
2. Repeat step 1 on the opposite side.
3. Overlap one end of part B with both edges of the two sheets A. Seal the edges with contact cement. Clamp the top edges together with the clothespins.
4. Tack the bottom of sheet B to the wooden base at evenly spaced intervals.
5. Repeat step 4 with remaining bark sheet B.

Adding the Top Rim

1. Using the hole punch (or awl), make holes along the top rim of bark sheets A and B, 1" down from the top and approximately 2" apart.
2. Gently bend one C branch into an oval and fit it carefully inside the top side rim. Clamp the branch to the bark with clothespins to hold it in place until the lacing is completed.
3. Join the bark to the oval branch rim using split bark or vine, by lacing through the holes diagonally over the branch and through the bark.

Adding Handles and Trim

1. Using one length of split bark E, form the handles by wrapping E around the rim C at either side and around itself as pictured. Sew the ends together with heavy thread if desired.
2. Wrap the circumference with trim E, and stitch it to the bark at various points with heavy thread.

GRAPEVINE BASKET

These easy-to-make baskets are as useful as they are attractive, and can add a
personal touch to any room. Baskets have always helped to express the heritage of native peoples, and pioneer householders cherished them for their usefulness. Antique baskets command high prices, while imported varieties are common
sights at discount stores. I cannot imagine a home that would not benefit from
adding a few choice baskets. Make several of these vine and wire frame baskets to
cover flowerpots or a glass jar filled with water and garden-fresh flowers.

MATERIALS

You will need a wire lampshade frame along with a selection of supple local vines,
such as Virginia creeper, grapevine, or honeysuckle.

TOOLS

♦ Garden shears or clippers

DIRECTIONS

1. Using the narrow end of the lampshade frame as the base, begin weaving the vine under and over the first wire rib. Continue to weave under and over each adjoining rib, as shown in drawing. If your frame has fewer than five spokes, add more by wrapping a length of heavy gauge wire tightly, using pliers, around the top and bottom rims of the shade frame, following the vertical line of the existing spokes.

2. For small projects, continue to weave in this fashion until completed. Check your progress as you go along and push each row of weaving up toward the top of the wire frame to ensure a tight weave.

3. For larger projects, follow the directions given for the lampshade on page 236.

4. When all rows are completed, wrap a length of vine in diagonal loops under and over the last two rows of vine, incuding the wire rim of the shade frame, as shown in drawing.

Finishing

Both the lampshade and vine baskets require no finishing. The vine's natural coloring provides a delightful rustic element. If, however, you want to incorporate these vine shades and baskets into a decorating scheme, splash them with an accent color. You might try first painting a basket white and then dashing flecks of dark paint here and there for effect.

Bark-Covered Basket
or Cheese Box

To make this basket, you will need to first obtain a round wooden cheese box. This may require some scouting on your part. Cheese is still shipped to stores in these boxes, so I would suggest checking with your local cheese shop first. Another good source might be garage sales, thrift shops, or flea markets.

MATERIALS

You will need one willow, alder, cedar, or other pliable branch for the handle, 42" long and 1" in diameter; one round wooden cheese box (or any similar wooden container), approximately 5" high and 15" in diameter; and enough peeled birch bark (or other peeled bark) sheets to cover the box. (If necessary, refer to instructions on how to peel the bark.) You will also need two galvanized box nails (#2p) and two 1½" flathead countersunk wood screws.

222

TOOLS

- ◆ Clippers or garden shears
- ◆ Sharp knife
- ◆ 1" wide straight wood chisel (required for bark peeling)
- ◆ Wooden mallet (required for bark peeling)
- ◆ Ruler or measuring tape
- ◆ Marking pencil
- ◆ Contact cement
- ◆ Spring-type clothespins
- ◆ Hammer
- ◆ Drill and bits
- ◆ Safety goggles
- ◆ Work gloves

DIRECTIONS

Applying the Bark

1. Measure and cut the bark sheets to fit the outside of the cheese box. You will probably have to fit several sheets together. Try to use as few as possible for a smooth look.

2. Lay the bark sheets face down on a worktable. Working in a well-ventilated room, apply the contact cement to one area of the outside of the cheese box. Apply the contact cement to the inside of an equal area of the bark and press the cemented areas together. (Work on small areas when gluing. Do not try to cover too much area at once.) Using the clothespins, clamp the top rim of the bark to the cheese box.

3. Continue cementing and clamping the bark sheets to the cheese box until it is completely covered. Allow the contact cement to dry for 24 hours.

Adding the Handle

1. Gently bend the 42" pliable branch into a U-shape. Using the garden shears, trim the ends of the branch so that they are even. Drill pilot holes into the two ends of the handle.

2. Fit the handle inside the cheese box at opposite sides. Drill pilot holes through both sides of the handle, 4" up from the bottom of the handle and part way into the cheese box. Nail in place using the box nails.

3. Turn the box on its side. Drill pilot holes from the bottom of the box at the two points where the handle ends meet the box bottom, being sure to meet the pre-drilled handle pilot holes. Join the bottom of the basket to the handle using wood screws.

4. Remove clothespins, checking to ensure that the cement has held.

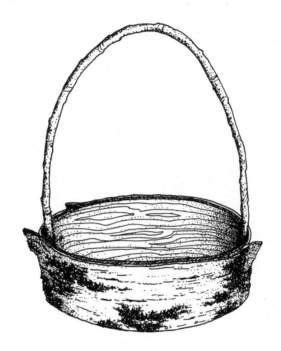

Finishing

This beautiful basket reflects the decorative and functional design elements of early native crafts. Use your basket to serve mounds of hot, crusty rolls at a buffet dinner, or to show off pots of herbs at a spring luncheon. Fill it with yarn or rag balls for rug making in the den. When you see how quickly you can make these cheese box/bark-covered baskets, you will want to make them in several sizes for yourself and for friends.

SMALL BARK-COVERED FRAME

Simplicity is the magic ingredient that permits the texture of the frame's bark to show. While bark-covered frames can be made in any size, the following directions are for a frame that is 12" x 14", with an inside opening that is 8" x 10". These frames make the perfect display for vintage needlework, as well as for family portraits.

MATERIALS

You will need an assortment of peeled bark sheets, at least 3" wide, along with one 12" x 14" flat-edged wooden picture frame with an 8" x 10" opening (this may be ready-made or homemade), glue, and ¾" carpet tacks.

TOOLS

◆ Scissors

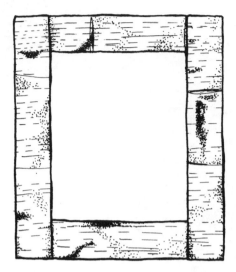 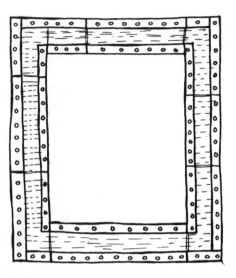

DIRECTIONS

Lay the wooden picture frame face up on the worktable, along with the selection of bark sheets. Make sure your bark sheets are flat. If they are curled, press them between heavy boards or bricks for a few days to smooth them. At this point, make sure the sheets of bark are wide enough to wrap around the edges of the frame. The bark will be tacked onto the frame at the back. Using the scissors, trim the ends of the bark sheets so they are straight. Select pieces of bark sheet and place them on the frame until you have a pleasing arrangement. Place a drop of glue on the back of each piece of bark to hold the pieces in place. Turn the frame over. With the front of the bark facing down and the back of the frame facing up, begin attaching the bark to the frame. Using the carpet tacks, tack the bark to the frame from the back by bringing the bark around the inside and outside edges of the frame. Wrap and tack in this fashion until the frame is completely covered.

GRAPEVINE AND WILLOW FRAME

This charming frame, with its 10" x 13" opening, holds a standard 11" by 14" precut mat. An antique grape print is especially nice, but any print becomes more captivating when it is shown off with a weaving of natural vines and tendrils.

MATERIALS

You will require a selection of branches, ranging in length from 5" to 21" and ¾" in diameter. You will also need a selection of grapevine branches or any other supple vine in lengths of at least 26". Galvanized flathead nails, sizes #2p and #4p, are also necessary.

TOOLS

- Crosscut hand saw
- Garden shears or clippers
- Ruler
- Pencil
- Hammer
- Drill with a selection of bits
- Safety goggles

GRAPEVINE AND WILLOW FRAME CUTTING CHART

NAME OF PART	QUANTITY	DIAMETER (INCHES)	LENGTH (INCHES)	DESCRIPTION
Parts A	2	¾	14	hardwood/ or pliable
Parts B	2	¾	17	hardwood/ or pliable
Parts C	2	¾	21	hardwood/ or pliable
Parts D	2	¾	23	hardwood/ or pliable
Parts E	4	¾	5	hardwood/ or pliable
Vine or grapevine branches	selection	–	26	supple

DIRECTIONS

Cutting the Branches and Vines
1. Cut two ¾" diameter branches for parts A, each 14" long.
2. Cut two ¾" diameter branches for parts B, each 17" long.
3. Cut two ¾" diameter branches for parts C, each 21" long.
4. Cut two ¾" diameter branches for parts D, each 23" long.
5. Cut four ¾" diameter branches for parts E, each 5" long.
6. Gather a selection of vines and cut into 26" lengths using clippers.

Assembling the Inner Frame

1. Butt the end of one part A against a part B, about 5½" up from the end of B.
2. Drill a pilot hole through B into A where they meet. Nail in place.
3. Repeat steps 1 and 2 with other parts A and B.
4. Lay the two A and B constructions on a worktable and arrange the parts, butting them against one another so that you form a frame opening of approximately 10" x 13".
5. At the points where A and B meet, drill pilot holes and nail in place.

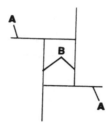

Assembling the Outer Frame

1. Butt the end of one part C against the end of one part D. Drill pilot holes and nail in place.

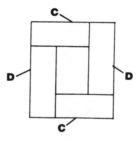

2. Repeat the preceding step with the other parts C and D.
3. Drill pilot holes and nail the two C and D parts together, forming a square that will become the outer frame.

Assembling the Frame

1. Place A and B construction (inner frame) on a worktable. Place C and D construction (outer frame) so that it fits around the inner frame. At the points where they meet, drill pilot holes and nail in place.

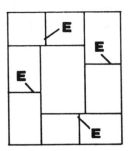

2. The remaining branches should be approximately 5" lengths for parts E. Drill and nail at the midpoints of the rectangles formed by the joining of the inner and outer frames.

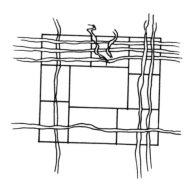

3. Weave the cut vines over and under the framework, filling in tightly.

Finishing

Left in its natural state, the grapevine and willow frame adds a degree of vintage charm to any setting. Painting the frame can accentuate a color scheme.

BIRCH BARK AND
WILLOW PICTURE FRAME

This is the most complicated of any of the frames because of its many parts, but the delightful result is well worth the extra effort. It is a good idea to gather more willow shoots than you need, since you may break a few at the beginning. The frame's interesting shape and natural bark markings will inspire you to choose a simple, bold piece to display in it. When in doubt, a mirror is always a good choice.

MATERIALS

Use such wood as birch, cedar, or beech. You will require lengths from 22" to 27", in diameters of ¾" to 1". You will also need pliable branches such as willow or alder, at

231

least 50" long and ½" in diameter, and a 12" x 17" piece of white birch bark. Other items you will need are a 12" x 17" mat board with an 8½" x 11" oval opening; contact cement; paper or cloth to protect bark while the project is in progress; 12" x 17" paper for a template; carpet tacks or heavy-duty staples; finishing nails (¾", 1", and 1½"); and heavy books or bricks for weight to press the bark. You may have the mat custom-cut at a frame shop or purchase one at a craft shop, or you may cut your own.

TOOLS

- ◆ Marking pencil
- ◆ Wood chisel and mallet
- ◆ Scissors or mat knife
- ◆ Sharp pocket penknife
- ◆ Single bit axe for felling trees
- ◆ Coping saw
- ◆ Crosscut hand saw
- ◆ Hammer
- ◆ Ruler or tape measure
- ◆ Electric drill with bits
- ◆ Safety goggles

DIRECTIONS

Making the Bark Mat
Note: To peel the bark, see page 211.
  1. Spread the front or side of your mat, and the back side of the bark, with contact cement. Press the bark sheet and mat together firmly. Cover with paper or cloth for protection. Weigh down with bricks or heavy books.
  2. Allow mat and bark to dry for 24 hours.
  3. Using the scissors or mat knife, trim the bark to fit the mat at the outside edge and carefully cut the oval opening from the bark, making sure the bark and mat are bonded to one another.

Cutting the Branches and Willow Loops
  1. Cut two 1¼" diameter branches for frame top and bottom A, each 22" long.
  2. Cut two 1" diameter branches for frame sides B, each 27" long.

3. Cut four ¾" diameter willow or other supple branches for oval loop trim C, each at least 45" long.

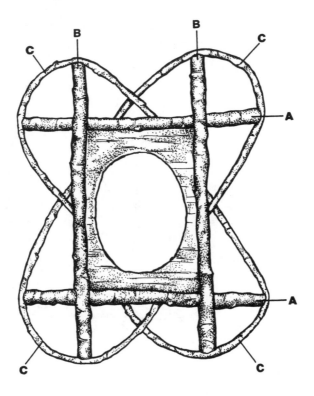

Laying Out the Main Frame
1. Decide which side of the branches will be the front of your frame. Using the 12" x 17" paper as a template, lay top and bottom branches A and side branches B along the outer edges of the paper to see how they will fit.
2. Using a pencil, mark the points on both sides of the branch where A and B cross, approximately 5" from the ends.

Cutting the Notches and Assembling the Main Frame
1. Using the crosscut hand saw, cut a notch between the pencil markings on the top of A and the bottom of B. Each notch should be only as deep as half the diameter of the branches so that the branches are flush when you fit them together.
2. Using the chisel, carve out each notch.
3. Fit pieces A and B together, adjusting the size of the notches if necessary.

4. With the back side up, drill a hole through the notched intersection three-quarters of the way through both branches. Do not penetrate more than halfway through branch B to avoid the nail heads showing from the front.
5. Hammer a nail through the hole at each intersection, making sure it is just short enough that it won't be seen.

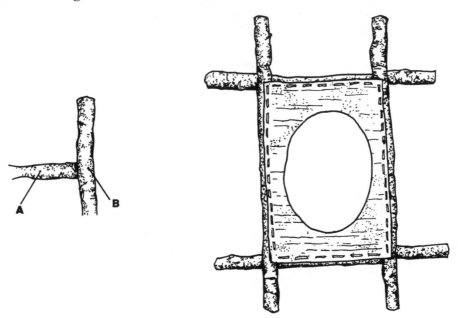

Adding the Birch Bark Mat
1. Lay the front of the frame face down on a sturdy worktable. Position the front of the mat over the back frame branches A and B.
2. Using carpet tacks or staples, tack the mat to the frame from the back.

Adding the Loops
1. Gently bend the willow twigs into arches.
2. Working from the back, choose a spot near the center of side branch B. Place the willow branch at this spot, letting about 1" of the willow hang over the mat. Drill a pilot hole through the willow loop trim into the frame branch. Nail in place.
3. Gently bend the willow outward so that it touches the two end tips of the main frame. Drill pilot holes and nail in place at these junctions. Continue bending, drilling, and nailing in place where it meets the center of top branch A.

4. Repeat with the other three willow branches, checking to make sure they are secured tightly to the ends of A and B. Your frame is now complete and ready for a picture, needlepoint, or mirror.

Finishing

The lyrical curves of the willow, combined with the subtle variations of the twig and birch bark markings, are best left in their natural state.

GRAPEVINE LAMPSHADE

This whimsical shade can help you turn a thrift shop find into an heirloom-quality lamp. Even if you have never done any other weaving, this technique is so simple that it is guaranteed to make you a proficient vine-weaver. Since finding just the right lampshade is often a difficult task, you can easily make your own and create a personal and decorative piece at the same time.

You will need a wire lampshade frame to serve as the base of your weaving. Rummage and garage sales often seem to have a good supply of old lampshades. Remove the old cloth and you have a fine base for your new vine shade. New wire frames can be purchased at craft shops, but the size and shape are usually not as interesting as some of the older ones. If your lampshade should have fewer than five spokes, you can add more. Take a length of heavy gauge wire and, using pliers, wrap it tightly around the top and bottom rims of the lampshade frame, following the vertical line of the existing spokes.

MATERIALS

You will need a frame that is 10" deep and 12" in diameter, or any other size for that special lamp. You will also require a selection of supple, local vine, such as grapevine, wisteria, or kudzu. To make your weaving easy, gather the vines in the summer, strip them of their leaves, and weave the green vines. When they dry on the frame, they will be very durable. If you have to use winter vines, soak them in warm water to make them flexible.

TOOLS

◆ Garden shears or clippers

DIRECTIONS

Lampshade frames usually have an even number of spokes, so the usual method of weaving "under and over" is not suitable for this project.

1. Begin at the top of the shade. Pull the first vine under one metal rib and over two ribs, carefully tucking the exposed ends under the rows of vine as you weave.

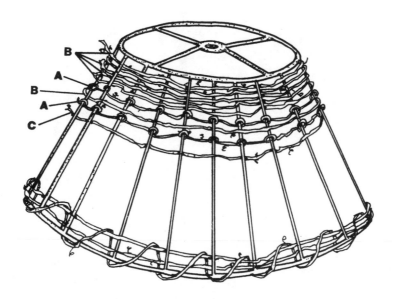

2. Continue this pattern for five or six rows.

3. With the end of a length of vine long enough to work comfortably with, pull the vine under one rib and loop it over the same rib. Moving in one direction, pull the vine under the next rib and loop it over that rib. Repeat this pattern until you have completed one row.

4. Begin the next row by pulling the vine under one rib and over two ribs. Push each row of vine-weaving up toward the completed weaving as you work, to ensure a tight weave.

5. Begin the next row, weaving under and over the same rib as in step 3.

6. Begin the next row, weaving under two and over one.

7. Repeat steps 4, 5, and 6 until you reach the bottom of the shade.

8. To complete the shade, wrap the vine in a diagonal loop under and over the last two rows of vine, including the wire frame rim.

NAPKIN RINGS

Awalk in the woods can lead you to loose scraps of bark that can be utilized
to make these charming napkin rings. They are great to use, or to give as
gifts. Making small items like these is also a good way to use up any peeled bark
you may have left over from some of the larger projects. For a unique house warm-
ing or shower gift, pack these napkin rings in one of your bark baskets, and tuck a
half-dozen homespun napkins inside.

MATERIALS

You will need peeled birch bark, 2" wide and 10" long (see pattern).

TOOLS

- ◆ Scissors and a sharp knife
- ◆ Hole punch (for Napkin Rings #2)
- ◆ Pencil and ruler

DIRECTIONS

Napkin Rings #1

Trace the outline of the pattern on the back of the birch bark. Using a pencil, mark the location of the two slits. Cut the bark to size with the scissors. Using a sharp knife, cut the two slits. Tuck the narrow end of the napkin ring into the first slit from the back, and then through the second slit from the front, so that the end is tucked inside the napkin ring.

Napkin Rings #2

Trace the outline of the pattern on the back of the birch bark and, using the scissors, cut out the shape. Using a pencil, mark the location of the two holes as indicated on the pattern. With the hole punch, make two holes in the bark. Cut another bark strip ¼" wide and 2" long. Turn the napkin ring into a circular shape, with the narrow end overlapping the holes approximately 2½" on the outside.

Thread the thin bark strip from the inside through one hole, catching the napkin ring tail under it. Thread it back through the remaining hole. The thin bark strip should be enough to hold the tail in place. If the tail comes loose you can add a drop of glue to keep it fastened.

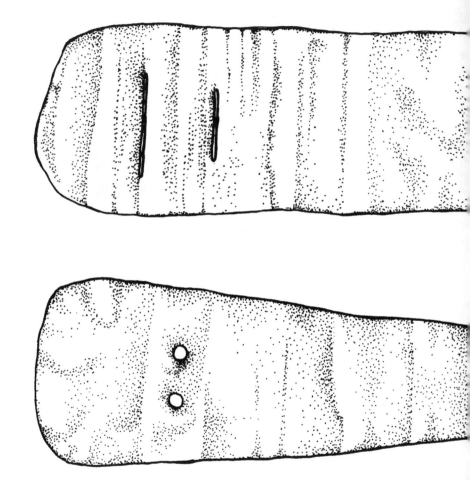

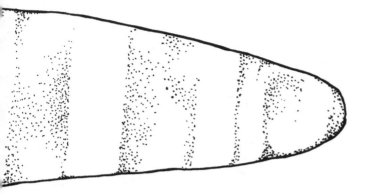

NAPKIN RING PATTERN

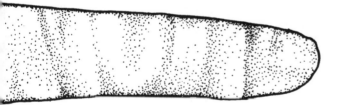